From Missionaries to Main Street

From Missionaries to Main Street

The Story of One Sgaw Karen Family
in the United States

Daniel Gilhooly

berghahn
NEW YORK · OXFORD
www.berghahnbooks.com

First published in 2023 by
Berghahn Books
www.berghahnbooks.com

© 2023 Daniel Gilhooly

Library of Congress Cataloging-in-Publication Data

A C.I.P. cataloging record is available from the Library of Congress
Library of Congress Cataloging in Publication Control Number:
2022036433

British Library Cataloguing in Publication Data

A catalogue record for this book is available from the British Library

ISBN 978-1-80073-808-9 hardback
ISBN 978-1-80073-809-6 ebook

https://doi.org/10.3167/9781800738089

This book is dedicated to the Htoo family and my mom, Audrey.

To the Htoos, thank you for sharing your stories and your friendship over the years. I am a better teacher, researcher, and person for having met you.

To my mom, thank you for the encouragement and support over the years!

Contents

Illustrations

Figures

Tables

Acknowledgments

I want to express my gratitude to all my friends, colleagues, and students who read some or all of the book and provided valuable feedback: Dawna Lisa Butterfield, Michelle Amos, Natasha Bertz, Jonathan Contreras, Chris Mu Htoo, William Wright, Collin Mills, and Jessica Gregory. And I have to offer special thanks to Nihal and Maria Khote for providing me the chance to teach the Htoos and other Karen families!

I also want to thank the entire Karen community in Sandville, GA. Your trust and friendship are greatly appreciated, and I look forward to the next ten years of our friendship and collaboration.

Abbreviations

ABAC	Abraham Baldwin Agricultural College
BDI	Biography-Driven Instruction
BIA	Burmese Independence Army
CBO	Community Based Organization
CLD	Culturally and Linguistically Diverse
DHS	Department of Homeland Security
DKBA	Democratic Karen Buddhist Army
DMV	Department of Motor Vehicles
DUI	Driving Under the Influence
EL	English Learner
ELA	English Language Arts
ELL	English Language Learner
ESOL	English to Speakers of Other Languages
GHSGT	Georgia High School Graduation Test
HBO	Home Box Office
INGO	International Non-governmental Organization
IOM	International Organization for Migration
IRB	Institutional Review Board
IRC	International Rescue Committee
KACF	Karen American Communities Foundation

KBC	Karen Baptist Convention
KBCUSA	Karen Baptist Churches of the United States of America
KCBO	Karen Community Based Organization
KECD	Karen Education and Culture Department
KHRG	Karen Human Rights Group
KNLA	Karen National Liberation Army
KNA	Karen National Association
KNU	Karen National Union
KRC	Karen Refugee Committee
KTWG	Karen Teachers Working Group
KWO	Karen Women's Organization
NGO	Non-governmental Organization
OIS	Office of Immigration Statistics
OWI	Operating While Intoxicated
PAR	Participatory Action Research
RTG	Royal Thai Government
SKBC	Sandville Karen Baptist Church
SLORC	State Law and Order Restoration Council
SNAP	Supplemental Nutrition Assistance Program
SPDC	State Peace and Development Council
TBC	Thai Border Consortium
TBBC	Thai Burma Border Consortium
UNHCR	United Nations High Command for Refugees
USCRI	United States Committee for Refugees and Migrants
VOLAGS	Voluntary Organizations
WIDA	World-Class Instructional Design and Assessment

Introduction

This book is the product of my eleven-year (2010 to 2021) and counting relationship with the Htoo (Gold) family, a Sgaw Karen family resettled to the United States in 2007 via the US refugee resettlement program. The Htoo family represents one of the approximately 180,000 refugees resettled to the United States under the designation Burmese.[1] This longitudinal interpretive biography[2] spans the Htoo's journey from their native Burma[3] to Thai refugee camps, their initial resettlement to the United States, and their current home in Sandville, Georgia (pseudonym). Throughout this book, I focus on what Norman K. Denzin calls "turning-point moments"[4] for me as a researcher and those turning-point moments for the Htoo family. Chapters 1 and 2 also consider the key historical turning points for the Karen people more broadly.

This book aims to provide teachers and others working with the Karen people with a resource about Karen culture and history through the individual and collective stories of one Sgaw Karen family. In discussions with teachers and others across the United States, it is clear that many lack awareness of their Karen students' backgrounds. This story provides some background on Sgaw Karen culture, history, and language against the backdrop of the Htoo family's story that I hope will provide readers more context.

This account also aims to provide some context to the current debate in the United States and around the globe surrounding refugee resettlement. This biographical portrait brings to light the experiences of the broader Karen diaspora and other resettled refugee communities resettling in the United States from Burma and beyond. Though the Htoo family story is singular, their experiences fleeing Burma, two-decade internment in Thai refugee camps, and their experiences resettling in the United States are characteristic of other resettling refugee families.

I also hope this book may stand as a historical document of the Htoo family during the early days of their American experience and provide future generations a sense of their family's first years in the United States. It may also be of interest to future generations of Gilhoolys who show interest in my story with the Karen people.

Finally, this story of Htoos hopes to offer readers some insight into the ways teachers can serve the dual roles of teacher-researchers. The lessons I learned through the process of teaching and researching alongside the Htoo children and other Karen children may serve as models for others working in similar capacities as in-home tutors or as classroom teachers. The successes and mistakes I have made along the way also offer important insights for others working in similar capacities.

Importantly, this is a very personal narrative and discloses personal information about the Htoo family members. I have repeatedly asked each of the Htoos about using their real names, and all agreed that it was important to include their names and forgo using pseudonyms. When I last asked Brown Htoo (December 2020) about this, he exclaimed without hesitation, "It's history!"

Note to reader: The Sgaw Karen people do not have surnames. However, when the family arrived in the United States, their names were adapted to fit American conventions. The final "word" in their name acts as a surname. For example, the patriarch is named Brown Htoo, while the youngest son is Ler Moo. This, as you can imagine, poses Sgaw Karen individuals and families many logistical issues. The Htoo family is relatively lucky that five of the eight family members share a common word that acts as a surname in the United States, Htoo. For readability, I will refer to the family collectively as the Htoos.

I have elected to maintain the pseudonym Sandville in reference to the Htoo's Karen community in rural Georgia. I maintain this pseudonym to keep the community's location anonymous and in line with other publications that refer to the community as Sandville.

Background

Meeting the Htoos

My introduction to the Htoo family was serendipitous. I finished my first year as a doctoral student when I was unexpectedly offered a much-needed summer employment opportunity. A classmate's wife worked for the Georgia Migrant Education Consortium. She was looking for a tutor for thirteen culturally and linguistically diverse (CLD)[5] learners

Table 0.1. The Htoo (Gold) Family (2011) © Daniel Gilhooly

Name	Name in English	Year of Birth	Place of Birth	Age upon Arrival in United States
Brown Htoo (father)	Brown Gold	1953	Myaungmya, Burma	53
Esther Htoo (mother)	Esther Gold	1962	Kawkareik, Burma	45
Sar Ah (female)	Sarah	1985	Myaungmya, Burma	22
Moe Tha Wah (male)	Life Heart White	1988	Myaungmya, Burma	19
Sam Ber Htoo (male)	December Gold	1990	Borna Refugee Camp, Thailand (now defunct)	16
Hser Gay Htoo (male)	Sweet Good Gold	1992	Ta La Thaw Refugee Camp, Thailand	14
Hser Ku Htoo (male)	Sweet Cool Gold	1995	Mae La Refugee Camp, Thailand	12
Ler Moo (male)	Life Gold	1999	Mae La Refugee Camp, Thailand	7

from four families, ranging in age from five to nineteen. I was told that a community from Burma had applied for summer tutoring through the consortium. I accepted without hesitation and with great curiosity. I had no idea that the families I was about to meet were ethnic Sgaw Karen[6] and that they would define the next decade of my academic, professional, and personal life.

The Beginning

I met the Htoo brothers for the first time on 1 May 2010, on a cloudless spring day among the rolling hills of eastern Georgia (about twenty-five miles from the South Carolina border). My friend's wife, Maria, from the Georgia Migrant Education Consortium, met me at a local Wal-Mart, and we drove together to meet my summer students. On the forty-minute drive, Maria filled me in on what little she knew about the two homes we

Figure 0.1. The Htoo family (2011). Back row from left to right: Ler Moo, Hser Gay Htoo, Sam Ber Htoo, Hser Ku Htoo. Front row left to right: Brown Htoo and Esther Htoo. © Daniel Gilhooly

would be visiting. I was going to meet the students and, hopefully, their parents to create a summer tutoring schedule. Maria thought they were new to the area, and she knew little more than that one of the children had applied for tutoring services through the high school, so she assumed it must be one of the Htoo brothers.

The first stop would be the Htoo home, and the second would be a home shared by the three remaining Karen families. Maria had met them all a few weeks earlier and indicated that they all were excited that she had found them a summer tutor. Throughout the entire drive, I was struck by how far into the country we were going and wondered how families from Burma had ended up in such a rural setting.

Three curious but sheepish adolescent young men emerged from a small white house at the sound of our approaching car. After a brief introduction, we discussed our summer tutoring schedule, and we decided that we would meet twice a week for two-hour study sessions during their summer break. Sam Ber Htoo, the eldest of the three young men, was the only brother to speak with me that day, but each of them seemed nervous and excited about the prospect of having a diversion from their quiet summer days in rural Georgia.

On the drive home, Maria and I drove in relative silence as I went over the visits in my head. After I bade her goodbye in the Wal-Mart parking lot, I drove home knowing I had stumbled upon my doctoral dissertation topic and the purpose I had hoped for when deciding to return to pursue a Ph.D. in language and literacy. I was elated and nonplussed that the Karen people had returned to my life in such a way and at such a time. I felt a sense of destiny at play and, as I was later to find out, so did Brown Htoo.

My History with the Karen

Meeting the Htoo brothers that day was not my first experience with the Karen people. More than twenty years prior, I had my first encounter with the people I would only later realize were displaced ethnic Karen. In 1989, I was first introduced to the Karen people during my senior year of high school (coincidentally, the same year the Htoos fled Burma) on a trip to Thailand with my parents and older brother, Brendan.

The late 1980s were an infamous time for Burma and the region. The year 1988 saw the fall of one military junta and the rise of another. The aptly named State Law and Order Restoration Council (SLORC) took power from the long-ruling general, Ne Win, in a coup led by generals Saw Maung and Than Shwe.[7] However, it was the 8888 Uprising that gained world attention.

The 8888 Uprising (8/8/88; 8 August 1988) saw the brutal repression of student demonstrations, and, for a moment, Burma came out of the shadows and appeared on the world stage. However, at the time, I was woefully unaware that my comfortable hotel was less than a hundred miles from the longest ongoing civil war of the twentieth century. Burmese government troops were fighting multiple insurgencies from various ethnic minorities and political groups, and hundreds of thousands, like the Htoos, were being displaced internally and externally to neighboring Thailand.

In 1988, I was living in a war zone myself. From 1984 until 1989, I lived with my parents in Israel amid the first intifada (uprising). Each year my father's company paid for biannual R & R trips outside the country. That year we traveled to Thailand. While in Chiang Mai, we visited a border community of hill tribes[8] that represented the liberated zones that preceded the establishment of refugee camps or, more officially, the temporary shelters that have continued to protect Karen and other displaced Burmese minorities and dissidents who have fled their native Burma. The conditions of those makeshift villages and the smiles on the children's faces made an impression on me. They provided a first glimpse of the Karen people and the paradoxes that often defined the Karen story.

Nearly ten years later, I would meet the Karen people again while traveling in Thailand. From 1997 to 2003, I lived and taught English in South Korea and often traveled throughout Southeast Asia. I traveled with my buddy Roger during our winter holidays to tour Thailand, Cambodia, and Laos. Each trip ended with a weeklong stay at a small beach resort on Ko Samet Island, a ninety-minute bus ride from Bangkok. Like most tourist spots in Thailand, undocumented Laotians, Khmer, Karen, and other economic immigrants from the region worked as boatmen, cooks, gardeners, guards, and housekeepers. On one of our earliest trips in 1999, we met Chi, a seventeen-year-old Buddhist Pwo Karen man working at the resort.

Like so many undocumented Karen, Chi had crossed the porous border between Burma and Thailand for employment opportunities in Thailand after the death of his mother and his father's ordination as a Buddhist monk. Unlike the Htoos, Chi fled Burma not in fear of persecution but for economic reasons. Even though we shared no common language, Chi became our buddy over the next four years. At first, we sat silently together, smoking cigarettes and watching Premier League football on TV.

As the resort was almost always empty, Chi and Jeab, a Thai manager, became our closest companions. Over the next four years, we visited Thailand once or twice a year and always made an effort to see Chi and Jeab. With the help of Jeab, we were able to communicate, and together we spent many an evening drinking Singha beer, playing cards, looking up at the stars, walking the beach, squidding (fishing for squid), and talking. When I think back on it now, I wonder how we could communicate since I spoke no Thai or Pwo Karen and Chi was just starting to learn Thai and spoke no English. And although Jeab spoke excellent English, she could not speak any of the Karen dialects. Yet, our friendship seemed a natural part of the experience at that time and in that place.

I like to think my friendship with Chi was one of mutual curiosity, and through him, I would begin to learn more about the Karen people. Soon after meeting Chi, I realized his intelligence and resourcefulness. With each visit, Jeab would praise Chi for his fast acquisition of Thai, allowing us to communicate on a wider range of topics. He effortlessly picked up card games we taught him, and he won nearly every game and looked bored and unimpressed with his accomplishment. He was also skilled with his hands, and it was clear that despite his lack of formal education, Chi was precocious and had a natural intelligence and resilience that I admired and envied. I marveled at how he took each task assigned with the same easy grace. He unloaded a boatload of heavy supplies from the mainland with the same ease of movement when sweeping the frangipani-strewn paths between bungalows. Yet, such a calm countenance belied his precarious situation.

As an undocumented person in Thailand, Chi was always on guard in case of immigration raids by the Thai authorities. He and so many undocumented in Thailand live in perpetual fear of the inevitable police raid when they are forced to pay bribes or face deportation. He and the other undocumented Karen, whom he shared a bungalow with at the resort, had made an escape hole in the floor of their bamboo hut in the eventuality of a surprise raid. Yet, unlike many of his peers, Chi remained in Thailand for nearly twenty years without being detained, a testament to his wit and resourcefulness. He is now married, has two children, and recently built a house back in Burma. The dream of saving money and returning to Burma with some capital was realized. He now owns a fast-food chicken restaurant, and I am certain of his success. However, back in the early 2000s, he was a wide-eyed Karen youth who had little experience with the wider world and tried his best to save his money and stay under the radar.

On each visit, Roger and I would leave him dollars in the hope he would save or treat himself to something special. And each time we returned, he would proudly show us the gold he purchased with his savings. It was his way of showing us that he had put his money to good use. Gold has long been the currency of choice for those living within the margins of many societies, and Chi knew the safety and security of gold compared to the volatile Baht. And, as I would later learn, gold was easier to conceal.

Meeting Chi also allowed me to begin connecting the dots on the Karen story in the region. In the late 1990s and early 2000s, various Karen insurgency groups were still actively fighting the regime in Rangoon, and the war was a hot topic in both the Thai and international press. I first read about the Karen in the *Bangkok Post*. And because of Chi, I began to read whatever I could about the Karen people. I soon found that the international press was having a field day with two Karen brothers, Johnny and Luther Htoo[9] (no relation to the Htoos in this book).

The brothers were the infamous leaders of a band of Karen child soldiers known as God's Army. At that time (2002), the brothers were ten years old. It was purported that Johnny and Luther, protected by their bodyguard Rambo, were reincarnations of two Karen generals who had long fought the Burmese Army for a free Karen state. The brothers had taken on legendary status within the Karen resistance and international media for obvious reasons. The chain-smoking twins were reported to have magical powers that kept them and their band impervious to Burmese government bullets and landmines. Moreover, the brothers were professed Christians, Baptists no less![10] I was shocked, confused, and I was hooked. I read what I could. The brothers were infamous for their fighting ability, strict diet, austere lifestyle, and deep conviction that Jesus was their savior who protected them in battle. While Johnny and Luther Htoo seemed a far cry from my buddy Chi, I was intrigued by the Karen story and Burma, and in 2000, Roger and I began planning a trip.

In 2001, due to the ongoing skirmishes between the Burmese Army and one of the dozens of insurgent militant groups, much of Burma was off-limits to foreign travelers. Despite these limitations, we could visit on a three-week tourist visa. The Burmese authorities severely monitored our movements around the country, and we had a government-issued driver for our five-day foray out of Rangoon north to Bagan. Maung Maung (pseudonym) was a cool guy who gave us some experiences I am not sure the generals would have appreciated.

Along the way, he introduced us to friends who were forthcoming about their mistrust of the government and fear for the country's future. We were told of a government campaign of "kidnapping," or the forced conscription of young men from various ethnic groups to serve in the ever-growing Tatmadaw (Burmese Army). His friend told us about people he knew being "taken" from bus stops across the country and forced into military service as a means of creating what the generals called a more "unified" country. The friend also spoke of his fears for the future of his Burma. And, tragically but unsurprisingly, these fears were warranted as I watched as the Saffron Revolution[11] played out on TV and computer screens around the world only six years after our visit.

In October 2007, only one month after the Htoo family left Thailand for the United States, the Saffron Revolution saw another brutal crackdown on demonstrators; this time, the brutality included the repression of Burma's ubiquitous saffron-clad and revered Buddhist monks and novices who were leading peaceful mass marches through Rangoon. During our visit in 2001, tensions were simmering, and the pot had yet to boil over, but the signs were ominous.

The roads outside the cities were nearly empty of any travel other than military convoys, and in 2001, the government limited personal travel by putting a cap on daily petrol purchases. There was also a heavy military presence in cities and frequent roadblocks. I took audio notes of the trip, and I listened to them while writing this book as much to relive the adventure as to inform this book.

In 2001, all trips to Burma began dubiously. First, all travelers were compelled to exchange $200 for 200 Myanmar dollars—a currency unrecognized outside the country and only selectively accepted by hotels within Burma. It was a way for the government to add much-needed greenbacks to their coffers. Then, as we had been warned, our customs official asked for a "gift," and we dutifully handed over more dollars without having made it through customs. The airport was filled with warnings about photography and video regulations, and all our cameras were inspected to confirm we were not foreign press.

In 2001, Aung San Suu Kyi was still under house arrest, adored by so many within Burma, and was still a hero in the West, having won the Nobel Prize for Peace in 1991. Burma was under US and European sanctions, and our decision to travel there was not without controversy and consideration. Many travelers were boycotting Burma in protest of the military junta's brutal crackdowns in 1988 and their continuing atrocities against minority groups. Even Hollywood took notice of Burma with films like *Beyond Rangoon*[12] and later as part of the Rambo franchise.[13]

Most of the country, including the Karen state, was off-limits. Attempts at bribing Maung Maung to take us into Karen state were met with stern rejections. However, we were able to meet some Karen. Our first brief encounter came at a train station outside Kalaw, Shan state, while on a three-day trek. A nineteenth-century British train stopped just as we were hiking into town. I clearly remember the look on those passengers' faces, and there was a haunting look in their eyes that stayed with me. And they seemed as taken with us; many rushed to the windows to get a glimpse of three white guys who looked equally wild and disheveled after a day trekking. Our guide later told us with some trepidation that it was a train bound to or from the Karen state and that people we had seen were most likely ethnic Karen.

During that trek, we had the chance to stay in Pa'O (Black Karen) villages. Walking the trails between villages and through patty fields, eating their food, and sleeping within their bamboo homes and Buddhist monasteries, provided me an experience that has colored my readings of the Karen people since and provided me some insights into the Karen story in Burma beyond my friendship with Chi and stories told to me by the Htoos and other Karen. Unlike other villages I had visited in the region, the Pa'O Karen would be my first experience with Karen reticence. Whereas in most villages in Southeast Asia familiar with tourists, children would approach us in large groups looking for candy or pens and laughing and screaming, these children kept their distance. When we approached a group returning from school to give them some pens we had brought, they stayed clear and were unwilling to come within fifty feet of us.

After that visit, I saw Chi one last time before leaving South Korea to return to the United States in 2003. He had left the island for the safety of crowded Bangkok, where he found old friends and a reprieve from the constant fear of police raids. It was much easier to remain anonymous in Bangkok than on a small island where illegal workers were fish-in-a-barrel for Thai police. He became a night watchman for a famous shopping mall in Bangkok, and we met for our last time at a local Bangkok park.

After I returned to the United States, I would receive a call from my mom every few months saying someone had called but all they would say was "Dan, Dan, Dan." I later came to find out it was Chi. Though we had (and have) kept up via Facebook, I had thought that Chi and the Karen people were no more than a fading chapter in my life. I had no idea that in 2006, Karen and other Burmese refugees had started resettling in towns and cities across the United States. Moreover, Burmese resettlement would represent the largest US resettlement program of the new millennium, with over 70,000 Karen alone resettling and an additional 100,000 ethnic Chin, Karenni, Burmese, Rohingya, and other ethnic minorities resettling to towns and cities across the United States (see table 0.2).

The Setting: Sandville, Georgia

From that first meeting with the Htoo brothers on 1 May 2010, until 13 July 2016, I was a regular visitor to the Karen community in Sandville, Georgia (the setting for much of my story with the Htoos). I first visited as an in-home tutor but soon became a researcher, cultural broker, collaborator, ad hoc caseworker, and friend of the Htoo family and two other Karen families that became the focus of my teaching and research.

From 2010 to 2012, the Htoo family was the primary focus of my research. Initially, I was researching them from the perspective of a teacher-participant observer, but in 2011, I collaborated on a research project with the three Htoo adolescent brothers—Sam Ber Htoo, Hser Gay Htoo, and Hser Ku Htoo. I was inspired by participatory action research (PAR), which led to our collaboration. This collaboration is described in more detail in chapter 4.

Methods

Through the various drafts and years of refining and rewriting this manuscript, I have come to realize that this is as much a story of me—the researcher, teacher, the white outsider, and friend of the Htoo family—as it is about the Karen people or the Htoo family members. And though this is not intended to be a purely academic text, I believe some description of what theories and methods informed me is important. My approach to teaching is better described in chapter 4.

My primary researcher role with the Htoo family was as a participant observer. As an in-home tutor, I observed their individual and collective

Table 0.2. Burmese and Karen Resettlement in the United States, 2006–2020. Data extracted from the Worldwide Refugee Admissions Processing System (interactive reporting). © Daniel Gilhooly

Year	Burmese resettled	Karen resettled
2006	2,294	1,993
2007	14,225	9,779
2008	19,000	12,588
2009	19,920	5,987
2010	17,176	7,417
2011	15,713	7,094
2012	15,112	5,455
2013	14,580	6,073
2014	15,971	4,892
2015	17,483	4,407
2016	4,078	2,224
2017	3,722	1,059
2018	3,711	1,065
2019	4,932	unknown
2020	2,115	unknown
TOTAL	181,604	73,373

learning styles and gained perspective on their home life and schooling. I had the chance to meet with and interview their English Language Learner (ELL) teacher multiple times. I also had access to all their transcripts, which helped me connect the dots of their educational experiences from their arrival in the United States throughout the time I worked with them. I also interviewed the brothers regularly during our two years together. But I was also a participant observer in so many other contexts where I accompanied them—at the grocery store, doctor's office, summer school programs, and at many Karen weddings, festivals, and within the homes of their friends and family.

I remember the first time I entered a convenience store with the brothers. Each stooped frozen beneath the neon lights, overwhelmed by this new space. Finding something to drink was far less familiar to them than I had anticipated. Such informal moments provided important perspectives on each of the brothers and their acculturation process. Over time, we went to Atlanta Braves baseball games, the movies, restaurants, and other excursions, and I documented everything. I filmed, took field notes, and made audio diaries from our first meeting until the writing of this manuscript.

Interpretive Biography and Friendship as Method

This book is modeled after what Norman Denzin refers to as interpretive biography.[14] Denzin defines interpretive biography as "creating literary, narrative, accounts and representations of lived experiences. Telling and inscribing stories."[15] My methods can best be conceptualized through what Lisa Tillman-Healy refers to as friendship as method.[16] Although I did not come across the work of Tillman-Healy until after I worked with the Htoo family, her ideas about friendship as method have since provided me a language that describes my ethnographic work with the Htoo brothers in particular.

Like any friendship, my relationship with the brothers took time, and I had to gain entry[17] into their world and include them in mine. This entrée was not easy due to the deference paid to teachers, especially white teachers, and our age differences created gaps. Yet, like most friendships, we bonded over shared interests, experiences, and inside jokes. Our love of sport gave us a starting point, and the role cane ball played in our friendship cannot be underestimated and is described in more detail in chapter 3 in my discussion on rapport.

Over time we began to talk more personally about relationships, fears, mistakes, and they would ask my advice on a range of topics. And they were my teachers of Karen culture, customs, beliefs, and language. And although these relationships formed naturally and differently with each brother, I was committed to the brothers meeting me as a whole person and not solely as a teacher. This bond helped create the kind of trust required in any such collaboration.

Another important aspect of friendship as a method is how friendships affect the actual fieldwork methods. In describing friendship as method,

Tillman writes: "our primary procedures are those we use to build and sustain friendships: conversation, everyday involvement, compassion, giving, and vulnerability."[18] Like all friendships, we had disagreements, but their willingness to challenge me was a sign that I had gained their trust and friendship over time.

Moreover, a longitudinal approach has enabled me the requisite time to understand the family and Sgaw Karen culture better and earn that trust. Importantly, the past ten years have allowed the Htoos and me the time to bridge our worlds, thus blurring simple binaries of teacher-student or researcher-participant. We were simultaneously friends, teachers, students, and collaborators.

Another aspect of this method for Tillmann-Healy is the time required to build friendships and how the relationships must build at the "natural pace of friendship."[19] One of the strengths of my research is the longitudinal nature of my work. My relationships with the Htoo family and the other Karen families I still contact regularly are lifelong. My prolonged hanging out with the Htoo family and other Karen families contributed to building relationships of *confianza*[20] or mutual trust that I have always viewed as being of paramount importance to teaching and collaborative research.

According to Lisa Tillmann-Healy, the last and most important aspect of this method relates to conducting research "with an ethic of friendship, a stance of hope, caring, justice and even love."[21] Tillmann-Healy continues: "Friendship as method is neither a program nor a guise strategically aimed at gaining further access. It is a level of investment in people's lives that puts fieldwork relationships on par with the project."[22] As I look back, I realize that this "investment" maybe my greatest strength as a researcher. I believed then and I believe now that by investing in their lives and serving them in various capacities I was putting their well-being "on par" with my own research goals. I had little idea of what research looked like at the time, but I knew how to help as a teacher, cultural broker, driver, English speaker, teacher, and friend. And over time, I think I have been a more ethical researcher and advocate of the Karen people.

My Interpretations

Similar to other interpretivist approaches, this book does not claim scientific neutrality nor hold any universal truths about the Htoo family or the Sgaw Karen people. Rather, through authentic and sustained relationships with Karen families, the following pages reveal relational truths[23] that we came together through our interactions as friends and collaborators.

This book is inherently subjective. I lay no claim to speaking on behalf of the Htoos or the wider Karen diaspora. In the following pages, I try to relate the many stories I was told and experienced with the Htoo family honestly and without embellishment. I followed certain protocols to substantiate my interpretations, choices of representation, and claims. Over time, these procedures evolved as I became a more sophisticated and conscientious researcher and writer.

While working on my dissertation, I came across the metaphor of crystallization used to describe the procedures I used to understand better or validate the multiple perspectives that I was able to draw from. Laurel Richardson writes of crystallization: "I propose that the central image for 'validity' for postmodern texts is not the triangle—a rigid, fixed, two-dimensional object. Rather, the central imagery is the crystal, which combines symmetry and substance with an infinite variety of shapes, substances, transmutations, multidimensionalities, and angles of approach."[24]

While I do not see this book as strictly guided by postmodernism, this definition of crystallization suits me as it seems to capture the multiple perspectives or vantage points that I was able to attain over the past eleven or so years. The Htoo brothers met multiple colleagues, friends, and family members who could hang out with the Htoo family and me throughout our time together. Such meetings not only strengthened our relationship but also provided new insights and "alternative interpretations."[25] Since I was working with an ethnic/cultural group different from my own, the wisdom of other ethnicities, genders, races, and ages proved invaluable in disrupting my interpretations, assumptions, and biases.

I also made a concerted effort to include the Karen brothers in my life. I am especially indebted to my Asian friends and colleagues who offered invaluable interpretations of cultural behaviors and mores that often demystified some of my interpretations and confusion.

During the years I worked with the Karen of Sandville, I had close Korean friends with whom I would often discuss my research and they would continually educate me on Asian cultural practices. For example, one day during a break in teaching, as I sat writing some field notes, I witnessed a grandfather talking to his baby grandson in the harshest of tones, and it struck me as at odds with what I knew about interacting with a baby. I thought, "What a grump!" None of the gentle cooing or silly talk I associated with talking to a baby was evidenced, and it struck me as somewhat cruel. After talking about this with one of my Korean friends, I came to find out that Korean culture has the same tradition. It seems that speaking harshly is a means of tricking evil spirits. It is believed that babies are vulnerable to evil spirits, so by speaking harshly, you fool the spirits—no spirit would want anyone who was being spoken to so harshly.

Although I was not married at the time and my wife has had minimal interactions with the Htoo family, she has worked with other Karen families and has been instrumental in helping me. As a Singhalese woman, she has also helped me better understand Karen culture, the effects of colonialism, the challenges acculturating, and what it is like to live through civil war.

While friends and colleagues would provide me with new insights, the literature on the Karen provided me broader context on the Karen story. Not long after speaking to my Korean friend about the grandfather, I came across this passage from Harry Marshall's 1922 study of the Karen. He writes:

> Nicknames of a special class are those given by parents to disguise their love of, and their satisfaction in, their offspring, in order to keep the demons away from the latter. Such names suggest parental contempt and lack of affection in the hope of deceiving the evil spirits into thinking that the parents cannot be injured through the injury or loss of their children. This practice is illustrated by names like Stink-pot, Rotten-fish, Lame-dog, etc., which often stick with men for life.[26]

After reading this passage, I asked the brothers about such a practice, and they asked their dad, and a new conversation would emerge. I found these kinds of dialogic interactions important for confirming information. They also became a means for the brothers to learn more about their culture from their father. This was a fascinating aspect of our collaboration that I had not envisioned.

These external audits[27] with colleagues and friends led to reflexivity and member checking.[28] I turned to the Htoo brothers for clarification throughout our time together and throughout the writing of this book. As I transcribed, read, and reread the corpus on Karen history and culture, looked over my field notes, watched video recordings we had made, read and reread transcripts, and discussed with friends and colleagues, more and more questions arose. I discussed my reflections, assumptions, questions, and confusion with the brothers and other family members via texts, emails, and video chats.

A critical component of this manuscript and other works I have written on the Karen is the use of various modes of data. The use of video and audio served the dual function of data preservation and multimodal representations of data. The brothers' perspectives were captured via what, who, and when they chose to film. A collection of their videos and the videos of other Karen youth is available on the Internet.[29] This video is an important visual and audio companion to this book.

I have also conducted formal and semi-formal interviews with the Htoo brothers, their father, Brown Htoo, and their mother, Esther, less frequently. From May 2010 to May 2012, I visited the Htoo home more than 150 times. At visit 151, it seems I stopped counting, and subsequent visits are solely labeled by date rather than by visit number. These visits lasted between three and ten hours. These interactions provided me rapport with the family and access and acceptance to the other Karen families in the area. I was and continue to be the "camera" guy, the white guy who can play cane ball to many Karen in the area. I was also a regular attendee at all community events such as weddings, church events, and other Karen celebrations from 2010 to 2016. However, for the Htoos and the other two families I tutored, I was Mr. Dan or Thera Dan (teacher Dan).

The Htoo family gave me access to paperwork the family possessed. I was able to take photographs of all their paperwork from the International Organization for Migration (IOM), which helped in their resettlement from the Thai camps to their first destination in the United States. These documents were the family's only official records before arrival. They were among their most treasured and guarded possessions, and I am forever grateful that they allowed me such access. It confirmed key dates and other data related to their resettlement application. I also collected all the Htoo brothers' school records from their schools in Phoenix to their respective graduations from high school. Transcripts, schoolwork, and other writing assignments they completed became important artifacts that chronicle their language development and attitudes and opinions on a host of issues. Each of the brothers was encouraged and motivated to write about their experiences. These biographical writings were important sources of information. Through these writings, I learned more about their lives before arriving in the United States and their feelings about school and life in the United States.

My extensive reading also informs this book on the Karen people. As the example above illustrates, the literature was often a source of information that led to the family's interesting and provocative questions. Over the years, I have read much of the corpus of English literature on the Karen, from missionary accounts to more contemporary academic accounts. Reading about the Karen became an obsession of sorts, and I relished in the nineteenth-century missionary accounts and more contemporary academic and non-fiction accounts.

I have also made a concerted effort to read as many Karen authors as possible. This includes the important writings of San C. Po, The Venerable Asanda Moonieinda, Ardeth Thawnghmung, and Violet Cho and the autobiographies of General Smith Dun, Saw Spencer Zan, Zoya Phan, and the more recent co-authored biographies of Saw Ralph and Naw Sheera.[30] I am also indebted to scholars who have spent much of their professional lives studying the people called Karen: Yoko Hayami, Martin Smith, Ashley South, and the late Dr. Ananda Rajah.

This book has morphed over the years in terms of goals and scope. Since 2016 I have taught pre-service and in-service teachers about working with

CLD learners. In many ways, they have become my target audience. My work with the Htoos colors how I teach my American students, providing examples that my students seem to appreciate. In many ways, the Htoo family's educational experience in the United States is similar to other CLD students' and families' experiences. Drawing on my experience with the Htoos has helped shape my current enthusiasm for biography-driven instruction (BDI)[31] as a means to culturally responsive teaching. More about my teaching approaches are addressed in chapters 4 and 5.

Finally, throughout the writing of this book, I have continually checked and double-checked my facts with the family via online chats, phone calls, and biannual visits. However, despite my attempts to verify all my "facts," I must confess to my reader that verification of some information was often met with added layers of confusion. This was primarily due to language barriers, the memories of the storytellers, or my misunderstanding or misinterpretations. One example relates to a story first recounted to me in 2011 about the power of tattoos and the story of Uncle James, a notoriously brave and "untouchable" Karen fighter who, it was related to me in 2011, had a stomach tattoo that protected him from Burmese bullets.

The Follies of Cross-Linguistic and Cross-Cultural Interactions

When I recently called Hser Ku Htoo to confirm my notes on this story, he asked his aunt Htoo Htoo (James's sister-in-law), who was conveniently visiting his home at the time. I simply asked where James's tattoo was located on his body as my field notes were unclear. I could overhear him ask his aunt and the ensuing silence made my stomach drop. It was clear she was unsure what I was talking about. After some reflection, she indicated that James had no such tattoos and then reconsidered and decided that such a tattoo existed but that it was hidden! This invariably led down another rabbit hole as it was difficult to qualify what she meant by a hidden tattoo or if her nephew's interpretation may have been off. I was able to verify from James's daughter that her father indeed had multiple visible tattoos but was never able to confirm that they were the source of his magical shield. However, everyone agreed that James had some form of protection from Burmese bullets.

I have tried to avoid including such stories throughout. Still, such examples speak to the inherent confusion when the interviewer and interviewee do not share a common language or culture and how memory and stories change over time. We also did not benefit from a trained Sgaw Karen-English interpreter, a major limitation of this study and addressed in the epilogue.

Note to the Reader: An Unexpected Turn

I have found it difficult to write the Htoo story in chronological order as I had anticipated, and I realize this may confuse the reader. This story provides information about all the Htoos at different stages of their lives, but the focus was those dates when I worked with them directly (2010–2012). For example, I have found it hard to include the three years the Htoo family lived in Iowa, so I have decided to provide my reader some sense of the family chronology in advance (see table 0.3).

As noted earlier, I taught the brothers weekly from 2010 to 2012. In 2012, we were studying and collaborating on research when, quite unexpectedly, they informed me that the family had decided to move to Des Moines, Iowa. Sarah, the eldest of the Htoo children, was living in Iowa and was buying a house in Des Moines, intending to bring the Htoo family together again under one roof. So, on 2 May 2012, at the request of Brown Htoo, I rented a U-Haul, and we packed the Htoo home and made the sixteen-hour drive north to Iowa.

After the Htoos relocated to Des Moines, I remained connected to them once or twice a year. I continued to work with the Karen community in Sandville but limited my teaching and research focus to two Karen families I taught. From 2012 until I left the area in 2016, I visited these two remaining Karen families two or more times per week and engaged in all manner of activities. When my funding for tutoring ran out in 2014, I continued to teach but much less formally.

I became what the children called Tee Wah (White Uncle). I wanted to provide the younger children (ages ten to sixteen) experiences with English beyond school limits. It was clear that they lacked any non-religious English socialization out-of-school, and I wanted to fill in that gap with the types of activities I enjoyed doing with all my nieces and nephews and thought would be meaningful to them.

As an uncle of sixteen nieces and nephews, this avuncular role suited me perfectly. Importantly, since my tutoring services were no longer funded, I felt a degree of freedom to create a learning atmosphere built around activities. Thus, these weekly sessions consisted of hiking, fishing, museum visits, tours of my university, the movie theater, the zoo, sporting events, and trips to the beach. These experiences helped me continue my research within the community and have informed all of my work on the Karen since.

Upon leaving the area in 2016, I began writing this book. I have continued to visit the Karen of Sandville, including the remaining Htoos, at least once a year.

Table 0.3. Htoo family residences (1990–2020) © Daniel Gilhooly

Date range	Place of residence	Family members
1990–2007	Mae La Refugee Camp, Thailand	Brown and Esther, Sarah and five male children
2007–2010	Phoenix, AZ	All except for eldest child, Sarah
2010–2012	Sandville, GA	All except for Sarah
2012–2015	Des Moines, IA	Brown, Esther, six children and three grand children
2015–present (2021)	Sandville, GA	Brown, Esther, Hser Ku Htoo, Ler Moo
2020–present (2021)	Des Moines, IA	Sar Ah, Moe Tha Wah, Sam Ber Htoo, Hser Gay Htoo

Organization of Chapters

I view the chapters of this book to be discrete, and they can be read independently. Chapter 1 will provide readers some insight into the Karen people and their history, culture, language, and diaspora. This chapter describes the major events that have impacted the Karen people, primarily the Sgaw Karen, over the past two centuries. The chapter attempts to draw parallels between the Htoo family and their Karen community in the United States and Karen traditional practices, beliefs, and customs in Burma.

Chapter 2 begins with the backstory of the Htoo parents, Brown and Esther, in relation to more contemporary Karen historical events. I relate Brown Htoo and Esther's story based on our multiple interviews and informal conversations. This will include a description of their early years and inevitable flight to Thailand. The chapter describes life in the camps, the resettlement process to the United States, and the Htoo's arrival in Phoenix.

Chapter 3 focuses on the Htoo experience in Sandville, Georgia, from 2009 to 2012 with an account of the development of the Karen community of Sandville, Georgia. The chapter concludes with an overview of my process of gaining rapport.

Chapter 4 focuses on our studies and portrays their lives when I was a regular visitor. The chapter also provides accounts of our research collaboration and our studies from 2010 to 2012.

Chapter 5 focuses on each of the Htoo brothers. The chapter looks specifically at their schooling experiences, English language development, and updates on each of them up until 2021. The focus here is on the four brothers I knew best.

The conclusion offers some final thoughts about the Htoo story and implications related to refugee resettlement, education, and a consideration of some of the limitations of my work.

Notes

1. Burmese is the generic term used for all refugees regardless of ethnicity resettled from Burma.
2. Denzin, *Interpretive Biography*, 11.
3. I use the name Burma throughout rather than the official name of the country, the Republic of the Union of Myanmar, out of respect to my Karen friends who prefer the appellation Burma.
4. Denzin, *Interpretive Biography*, 22.
5. I use the term culturally and linguistically diverse (CLD) learners throughout rather than the more common labels English learners (EL) or English language learners (ELL) as CLD incorporates the culture of students as an important consideration.
6. I use the terms Sgaw Karen and Karen interchangeably throughout. When referencing another a non-Sgaw Karen subgroup I will identify that subgroup rather than only using the appellation Karen.
7. Charney, *History of Modern Burma*, 185.
8. Hill tribes are considered by many to be a derogatory reference to the many ethnic minorities in northern Thailand, and I use those terms only because this is how it was advertised at the time tourists like my family visited the region.
9. Beech, "We Were Bulletproof."
10. Beech, "We Were Bulletproof."
11. Charney, *History of Modern Burma*, 19.
12. Boorman, *Beyond Rangoon*.
13. *Rambo IV* sees John Rambo along the Thai-Burmese border.
14. Denzin, *Interpretive Biography*.
15. Denzin, *Interpretive Biography*, 11.
16. Tillman-Healy, "Friendship as Method," 729.
17. Tillman-Healy, "Friendship as Method," 732.
18. Tillman-Healy, "Friendship as Method," 734.

19. Tillman-Healy, "Friendship as Method," 734.
20. Gonzalez et al., "Funds of Knowledge," 3.
21. Tillman-Healy, "Friendship as Method," 735.
22. Tillman-Healy, "Friendship as Method," 735.
23. Tillman-Healy, "Friendship as Method," 733.
24. Richardson and St. Pierre, "Writing: A Method of Inquiry," 934.
25. Stake, *The Art of Case Study Research*, 113.
26. Marshall, *Karen People*, 170.
27. Poduthase, "Rigor in Qualitative Research," 25.
28. Stake, *The Art of Case Study Research*, 115.
29. CMHtoo, "Karen Movie," 27 July 2021. https://vimeo.com/manage/videos/580045395.
30. Po, *Burma and the Karens*; Moonieinda, *The Karen People*; Thawnghmung, *Karen Revolution in Burma*; Cho, "Rearranging Beads"; Cho, "Searching for Home"; Dun, *Memoirs*; Zan, *Life's Journey in Faith*; Phan, *Little Daughter*; Smith, *Fifty Years in Burma*.
31. Herrera, *Biography-Driven Teaching*, 20.

Chapter 1

The People Called Karen

> We are the leaf, other races are the thorn; if the
> leaf falls on the thorn, it is pierced; if the thorn
> lands on the leaf; the leaf is pierced all the same!
>
> —Karen proverb

The only document provided to me by my employer listed each of the families I would teach, and next to each family member's name, it clearly stated "Burmese." I soon found out that such confusion was common when it came to working with the Karen in the United States. When I first met the Htoo family in 2010, there were a few online resources and academic articles on Karen history, religion, and the ongoing civil war, but I only found one site dedicated to working with Karen people in the United States, a site created by the Karen American Communities Foundation (KACF).

KACF is a non-profit organization established in 2007 to help "the Karen people of Burma survive the trauma of resettlement from a jungle war zone to an extremely dissimilar urban culture." That phrase stuck with me, and I wondered what traumas my families had faced. And I also wondered how the Karen families I was working with had ended up so deep in the rural Southern United States.

Over the past ten years working with the Karen community of Sandville (pseudonym), Georgia, I have realized that the Karen people are a discrete ethnic group with their own cultural practices, language, and very compelling history. Of the Karen families I met in 2010, some had only been in the United States for a few months and others, like the Htoos, for about 2.5 years. The more I read about the Karen, the more I realized how much of their culture was still intact and how similar my field notes were to the accounts written by missionaries two hundred years ago. There were days when I went to teach at one of the Karen homes, and it very much felt like

I was back in rural Thailand or Burma. The cocks crowing, relentless heat, the ubiquitous smell of rice, and burning wood were just the surface, and over time I have come to realize how I was able to observe a very singular story of refugee resettlement in the United States. While I am not a historian, I believe that to understand Karen families like the Htoos better, we must consider the historical and cultural context of the Sgaw Karen people more broadly.

Identifying the People Called Karen

The year 2013 marked two hundred years since the first American missionaries arrived in Burma. Although the Karen would not be the focus of early attempts at proselytizing (the early focus was on the majority Burman population), the arrival of Ann and Adoniram Judson marks a period of transformation for the Sgaw Karen people. This chapter aims to answer the following questions against the backdrop of the Htoo family's story.

Who are the Karen people? What are their origins? What are some key historical events that have impacted the Karen people? What are some of the Karen customs, beliefs, and ways of being that they have maintained in the United States? How have Karen relationships with American Christian missionaries and the British colonial enterprise impacted Karen culture and contemporary history? Why have the Karen people been fleeing their native villages in Burma? And, finally, why have the Karen people been resettling in the United States?

Karen Origins

Significantly, the appellation *Karen* (Kuh REN or kä-rĕn) refers to a diverse group that is neither bound by language nor other traditional markers of ethnicity. The Htoo family identifies as Sgaw Karen or White Karen, the largest Karen group.

The etymology of the word *Karen* is not without controversy. The earliest recorded Western ethnographic classification of the Karen people comes from the accounts of Marco Polo, who refers to Karen as *Carajan*.[1] In the late 1700s, Father Vincentius Sangermano, an Italian Catholic missionary serving in the region, offers the first detailed account of the Karen, referring to them as *Carians*.[2] Ethnic Bamar or Burmans, the ethnic majority group in Burma, expressed great contempt for the Karen, referring to them as "wild cattle of the hills."[3] The Sgaw Karen self-identify as *pgan gan yaw* (also spelled *pga k' nyau)* and the designation *Karen* does not exist in any of the Karen dialects.[4]

Brown Htoo translated *pgan gan yaw* as "human beings." Whatever its origins, the exonym Karen is symbolic of the historical objectification of the Karen people by others; neighbors, British civil servants, military personnel serving in Burma, foes, foreign missionaries, and outside academics.

Today, the Karen people are estimated to be either the second or third largest ethnic group in Burma. Due to the protracted civil war, it has been difficult to estimate the populations of each ethnic group residing in Burma.[5] The Karen National Union (KNU) has politicized the population, most likely overestimating Karen populations and the Burmese government, who most likely are underestimating how many Karen live in Burma. The Karen population in Thailand (Thai citizens) is more certain, with Thai-Karen representing the largest ethnic minority at approximately 430,000.[6]

Whenever Brown Htoo spoke of Karen origins, he invariably spoke of a Karen progenitor. Karen writer Saw Moe Troo describes Karen origins concerning the same Karen progenitor, Htot Meh Pah (also spelled Poo Tho Mae Pa, grandfather boar tusk) Saw Moe Troo writes:

> According to the tribal traditions of the Karens their earliest known patriarch is Poo Htot-meh-pah, boar tusk's father. Hence in answer to the question "Who is a Karen?" one of the answers should be (1) one who can claim his ancestry to Htot-meh-pah and (2) one who possesses, maintains and cultivates the legacies bequeathed to him by the said fore-bear and his predecessors.[7]

In terms of Karen cultural characteristics, Karen writers like Saw Moe Troo and Mika Rolley described the Karen people as adhering to the following nine precepts: "The knowledge that there is a God, the Divine Being; High moral and ethical standards; Honesty; Simplicity; quiet and peaceful living; Hospitality; language; National Costumes; and Aptitude for music."[8]

Other Karens are less clear in their classification and less willing to subscribe to the distinctly religious overtones of the above ethnic description of Christian Karen nationalists like Saw Moe Troo. According to the Venerable Moonieinda, a Karen Buddhist monk and writer living in Australia, one only needs to self-identify as Karen. He writes, "The Karen are unique in that it is not necessary to have Karen parents to be Karen. Many Karen say that to be Karen a person must identify as Karen; know Karen culture and customs, and speak a Karen language."[9] Such an approach to ethnicity exemplifies some of the confusion involved in identifying who is and who is not Karen. Such ambiguity may stem from the refugee camp experience where Sgaw Karen became a lingua franca bridging a variety of ethnicities and religions in the camps and thus blurring ethnic lines. The Htoo family introduced me to friends who they said were Karen despite their very different physiognomies. I have met self-identifying Karen men and women in the United States with radically different physical features, some seemingly originating from South Asia.

The Karen people are found throughout the plains of southern Burma to the hills along the Thai-Burmese border. Chris Cusano contends, "Karen is a blanket term that covers several peoples inhabiting a large area of mainland Southeast Asia between Burma's Irrawaddy River and Thailand's Chao Phraya [River]."[10] The majority of Karen people live on both sides of the central Thailand/Burmese border. Interestingly, Brown Htoo is from the Irrawaddy Delta, whereas his wife, Esther, is from Karen state some 550 kilometers to the east. Their marriage represents the intermarriage of lowland delta Karen with highland Karen, a biproduct of sixty years of civil war and the migration of lowland Karen east to the relative safety of the Karen state and/or Thailand. For scholars like Cusano, these intermarriages between lowland and highland Karen have created "a generation of culturally, linguistically, and religiously diverse Karens who personify the socio-demographic impact of the KNU eastern migration."[11] The Htoo children represent this mixed highland–lowland generation.

Any attempt at verifying the region of origin of the Karen people is also problematic. While there are Karen communities in both Thailand and Burma, some scholars argue the Karen people migrated into the region that is now modern Burma. Others believe the Karen are indigenous to the region and have rights to an independent state.[12] The reality is far less clear.

The lack of historical written records makes any claim spurious. Most Karen claim to be from the land of "running sand,"[13] which many scholars and Karen elders such as Brown Htoo believe to be either the Gobi Desert in China or Yunnan Province, China.[14] Brown Htoo often spoke of this "river of sand," but he was unsure if it was in China or elsewhere.

Despite the ambiguities related to the geographic origins of the Karen people, the Sgaw Karen, in particular, have had long historical ties with the United States and have been coming to the United States to study and preach since the mid-nineteenth century. It is surprising that Karen-American relations date back as far as they do. Karen-American interactions began as early as the 1820s when the United States was still fighting wars against the British, and there were only twenty-nine states in the union! This early historical connection means that the Karen people represent one of the first groups, beyond Europe, to have ties with the United States. Karen students were among the first to arrive in the United States as "international" students.

From 2006 to 2021, "Burmese" refugees represented the largest group resettled by the US government. Although multiple ethnic groups are re-

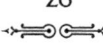

settling under the umbrella designation *Burmese* (i.e., ethnic Chin, Karenni, Burman, and Rohingya), the Karen people represent the largest ethnic group resettling. Of those resettling as *Burmese*,[15] 40 percent are listed as Karen, the majority of whom are Sgaw Karen[16] Despite linguistic and religious differences, the various Karen groups share many cultural practices.

The Htoos and their Karen community in rural Sandville, Georgia, have maintained many traditional practices. Their Karen community has promoted Sgaw Karen literacy, agriculture practices in planting and harvesting, sport, diet and cooking practices, foraging, hunting and trapping, traditional storytelling, and, most notably, religion.[17]

Karen Traditions

The traditional practices of many Karen in Burma, Thailand, and the refugee camps have not changed in centuries. Most Karen in Burma and Thailand continue to harvest rice since they settled in both the plains and hills. Depending on their geographical location, they practice both wet rice and dry rice cultivation.[18] They are noted for their skills in farming, hunting, lumbering, and soldiering. Their adeptness as mahouts (someone who works with elephants) was long renowned in the region.[19]

Though the Htoo children's lived experiences differ from their parents' childhoods, much of Sgaw Karen's social life has been preserved post-resettlement in the United States. According to Harry Marshall's 1922 Karen ethnography,[20] village life was synonymous with family life as the Karen people traditionally lived close to their affinal kin. Nuclear families and affinal relationships were, and are, highly esteemed among the Karen people. It was common for extended families to live together in a village longhouse[21] or closely situated bamboo homes. This pattern of living has continued after displacement in the refugee camps, where families like the Htoos lived close to extended family members. And such practices also continue for those Karen resettled in the United States, where apartment complexes are often home to families who had lived in the same zones only a few years earlier in one of the nine refugee camps in Thailand.

The Karen community in Sandville consists of more than thirty extended family members living within three miles of the Htoo family home. The Htoo's secondary migration story in the United States is indicative of other refugees in the United States[22] and previous Southeast Asian refugee groups.[23] The Htoos first decade in the United States was spent first in Phoenix, Arizona, then in Sandville, Georgia, and then Des Moines, Iowa, before finally settling back in Sandville. Many resettled Karen families share similar stories of transience as they move in pursuit of higher-

Figure 1.1. The extended Htoo family, Sandville, GA (2009). © Daniel Gilhooly

paying employment opportunities, family reunification, warmer weather, or community support. The entire Karen population of Sandville migrated to eastern Georgia after their initial resettlements in Arizona, New York, Kentucky, and North Carolina. Notably, such mobility is another traditional feature of Karen in Burma, who were nomadic[24] or seminomadic.[25]

Agricultural Practices

The Htoo community in Sandville, Georgia, still uses many of their traditional agricultural practices, and many of these skills are being passed to the younger generation. I argue elsewhere[26] that the passing down of traditional knowledge is one asset afforded the Htoos and other families living in rural areas in the United States. A rural lifestyle helps offset some of the generational dissonances that often occur in resettled families where children "acquire the language and skills of their new culture more quickly than their parents do, resulting in family conflicts."[27] In Sandville, I found children more connected to parents and grandparents as result of their rural isolation but also because traditional knowledge was being

passed down. One example from my experiences bringing a group of Karen children to the Atlanta Zoo highlights this traditional knowledge being passed down.

I had filled my car with five excited female Karen students that I worked with in addition to the Htoo family. It was "girls-day-out" with Mr. Dan. While I was able to attain free tickets for admission, I had little money to buy food and had not thought to bring any. As the girls got hungry, I searched for ways to possibly fill their bellies until we got home. I had no luck. When I returned to them, to my surprise, they were all picking something from what I soon realized was a fruit-bearing tree (I was never able to identify the fruit) and were happily munching down what looked like a crab apple. They said all they needed was some salt so I found some salt packets and the problem was solved! This led to new discoveries as I came to realize they could forage for many edible plants. Learning how to forage from elders is one of the ways traditional knowledge is being preserved in rural Sandville.

Community Elders and the Oral Tradition

Traditionally, elders played the important role of maintaining and preserving the village's history by memorizing and retelling oral narratives documenting the village's history.[28] These stories are passed down orally to ensure that the village's history and ancient legends and prophecies were retained by future generations.[29] These *htas* (oral stories) were, and remain an important means of preserving traditional narratives. Interestingly, I observed many similar narrative events when Brown Htoo, and other Karen elders, related family histories, myths, legends, and parables. Such storytelling events also served to pass on various traditional beliefs, reiterate the importance of maintaining Karen identity, stern warnings about the dangers of drugs and alcohol, and other temptations of American culture. But, most often, these stories reiterated the importance of accepting Jesus as your savior.

Traditionally, Karen elders were responsible for electing a village chief who acted as the village's patriarch.[30] Analogously, such a tradition continues within Karen communities in the United States who rely on elders for guidance, support, and the maintenance of cultural practices. In Sandville, Karen preachers and other elders hold similar positions and offer cultural, political, spiritual, and moral leadership. Brown Htoo is one such leader in the Sandville Karen community.

Karen missionaries from Thai refugee camps, Burma, and the United States keep US-Karen communities like Sandville connected to the wider diaspora with frequent visits to Karen congregations across the United States, Australia, Canada, and Norway. These Karen missionaries are usually representatives from various Karen Baptist organizations. They share information, teach Karen language and music classes, preach, collect moneys for multiple causes, apprise Karen on the latest events from Thailand and Burma, and provide information on a host of other secular, political, and religious issues. I had the opportunity to meet and talk with many of these guests when they stayed at the Htoos. Many were English-speaking religious scholars from one of the Christian universities in Burma or held important positions within various Karen Baptist organizations.

Community Life

Traditional Karen community life was egalitarian, with all village members sharing ordinary life tasks while little differences in class existed.[31] The land was considered free and belonged to the community.[32] Every family was at liberty to work as much land as they could tend, and the village worked cooperatively in harvesting and threshing. Marshall's observations of Karen's high regard for community over individuality is an important consideration when examining Karen resettlement in the United States. Marshall writes:

> There was little occasion for individual initiative among the Karen on account of the important part played by the communal activity amongst them. One could claim no particular credit for his deeds of blood on a raid. That belonged rather to the organizer and leader of the foray. One never set out on a journey or attempted any special work alone. In some sections it was the custom for the chiefs to blow a horn or beat a gong as a signal to go to the fields. Everyone went on that signal. None would go without it.[33]

Such observations are particularly striking when considering Karen resettlement in the United States, where individualism typically takes precedence over collectivism. In my experiences with the Htoos and other Karen families/communities in the United States, I noted the same collective action as Marshall describes exactly a century ago.

The Htoo home was a hive of activity. Adults organize religious and cultural events; plant or harvest together; hunt and butcher; sing, and pray. The collective spirit of village life has helped sustain and grow the Sandville community. The Karen community does not limit their collectivism to Karen friends and family and can be found lending a helping hand to members from the local Baptist church that has welcomed them. The Karen community relies on each other for transportation, loans, cutting and transporting wood, fixing and building homes and outbuildings, and in a multitude of different ways.

Like previous immigrant groups, such collectivism has helped in the resettlement process. Karen collectivism in Sandville has helped the

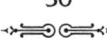

community establish itself and prosper. Each Karen home in Sandville is Karen-owned.

However, the claim that Karen communities are egalitarian does not resonate with my observations. Karen communities, like that of Sandville, have a hierarchy with pastors and their families bearing the most influence. Some children of parents who have less status often complain about these inequities. They indicated that this was due to their parents' lack of education and the power held by the educated. This very much aligns with other observations in the camps where Sgaw Karen Christian elites have power.[34]

Karen Dress

Many of the ethnic groups of the highlands of Burma were distinguished by their clothing. For example, Sgaw and Pwo are considered white Karen[35] due to the color of their dress. In the United States, Karen youth and adults wear their traditional Karen shirts and dresses at all-Karen events such as church services, Karen New Year's celebrations, and it has become a means for many in the United States to express their Karen-ness. Sam Ber Htoo spoke with me about why he wears his Karen shirt and carries his Karen bag regularly, and speaks to the continued importance of clothing as a means of ethnic identification.

> People don't know Karen. They just think I'm Chinese. That really what people think! But I'm proud Karen and I like to wear my people's shirt. I am Karen, not Burmese, not Karenni, Thai, not Chinese. I want people to know I'm Karen and not all those other people. For Karen people, we are proud to be Karen. And want to show everyone we Karen. And it important. Sometimes my school think I'm Burmese because all the paper say Burmese. And many people think we Thai because we live in Thai camp but we Karen people.[36]

Just as Karen clothing sets the Karen apart from other Burmese ethnic groups, the Karen love and involvement in music is another important aspect of Karen culture that is widely maintained in the United States and throughout the diaspora. Tellingly, the earlier quote by Karen writer Saw Moe Troo about Karen culture includes the role of music and deserves some account.

Karen and Music

As we shall see, Christianity has had a profound impact on Karen culture, and this is true for how Christianity has impacted Karen music. Harry Marshall's comprehensive ethnographic account of the Karen offers this description: "The Karen are lovers of music . . . Occidental music has taken

Figure 1.2. Karen Rockers (2013). © Daniel Gilhooly

such a hold of those who have become Christians that they have almost entirely given up their native music."[37] Two years later, in 1924, James Lewis offers his take on the Karen love of music that resonates today. "Considering their love and appreciation of music, it is safe to generalize and say that whichever language the Karen sing in, that is the one he loves better."[38] Today, YouTube is replete with Karen music videos. And while many are Christian songs, everything from love ballads to gangster raps are uploaded! Karen youth demonstrate a keen ability to write, record, and disseminate these music videos digitally throughout the diaspora.

The Htoo family is no exception. Brown, like most Karen men, plays guitar and sings. Sam Ber Htoo and Hser Gay Htoo are aspiring musicians who play together with family and friends in a band (see figure 1.2).

Karen Relations with the West

As noted earlier, Karen-American relations are long-standing, dating back to the early nineteenth century and the arrival of the first American missionaries, Adoniram and Anne Judson. The Judsons' arrival in Burma and subsequent work with the Karen represent the first Christian American missionary effort outside the United States.[39] The Judsons, Boardmens, and later missionaries achieved legendary status among American congregants stateside who had an insatiable appetite for the wild and exotic reports coming from these missionaries in far-off lands.[40]

In 1829, after the Judsons had spent nearly fifteen years trying, unsuccessfully, to convert the majority Buddhist Burman population who they originally had considered more civilized and capable of civilizing on their path to accepting Christ. The missionaries found the Karen people far more receptive. Kho Tha Byu, the first Karen convert in 1829, was responsible for the rapid rate of Karen conversion.[41] He is immortalized by Karen throughout the Karen diaspora with his own holiday in the third week of May.

Before accepting Jesus, Ko Tha Byu seems made in the mold of many a Catholic saint who experienced mighty transformations. Before accepting Jesus as his savior, he was a notorious murdering dacoit or bandit. Ko Tha Byu has become an archetype Karen convert. He is often referred to by wayward Karen hoping to change their lives or referenced as inspiration by the saved. Missionary accounts of Ko Tha Byu also describe his extraordinary gifts as a proselytizer. He is credited with making "the connection" between the Karen tradition of monotheism with the Judsons' Christianity.[42]

> A Karen called Ko Tha Byu, debt slave to a Burman, had been set free by Dr. Judson and employed as a water carrier. Ko Tha Byu found a Christian tract; its teachings struck him as singularly like the teachings of the God-tradition of his people. His eyes were open; he discovered that, at last, the long-predicted return to God to his nation through the white man had been fulfilled . . . he became the means of opening up to the American Missionaries a field of enterprise of which they had never dreamed.[43]

Judson and Ko Tha Byu stand atop the pantheon of Christians who continue to be honored within the Karen Christian diaspora. His transformation from wayward outlaw to proselytizing preacher also represents a major transformation of the Sgaw Karen people.

The Karen and Christianity: The American Missionary Enterprise

Christianity's impact on Sgaw Karen culture, history, language, Karen nationalist movements, and the eventual resettlement to the United States cannot be overestimated. Christian churches are the center of many Karen communities in Burma, the refugee camps, and throughout the Karen diaspora. This focus on Christian churches is no more evident than in Sandville, where the physical space of the newly erected Sandville Karen Baptist Church (SKBC) is the center of the Htoo community's religious and cultural life. Today, members of the Karen Sandville community send out their missionaries across the United States and beyond to carry on the mission established nearly two hundred years ago.

According to many Karen, such as Brown Htoo, "biblical" themed oral stories were passed down long before the arrival of missionaries. It seems that stories of creation, expulsion from the garden, the flood, Satan, and resurrection were popular Karen memes long before the arrival of Judson. What seems to have set the Karen apart was the belief in a single God (Ywa).[44]

According to Karen, such as Brown Htoo, the Karen were monotheists believing in one Ywa (God).[45] An ancient Karen *hta* (oral poem) tells how the Karen people had once possessed and then lost Ywa. And with the loss of Ywa came the loss of a book of wisdom once bestowed upon them by Ywa. Yoko Hayami relates this story told to her by Karen that resembles much of what Brown Htoo described to me over the years.

> Long ago, when Ywa was still with us, Ywa called all the children. Among them were the Karen, Burman, Thai, Chinese and the white brothers. The Karen was the eldest and the white brother the youngest. Ywa gave the Karen brother a Golden Book of wisdom. The Karen took it to his field, and left it on a tree stump. When he burned the field, the book was burned to ashes. Chickens came and walked over and pecked at the ashes. Another book of knowledge was given to the youngest white brother and that is why the white foreigners are so developed today. The other brothers picked the remains of the ashes and therefore today they have chicken-scratch letters of their own. Ywa departed, and the Karen have nothing for themselves except the bones of those chickens to consult.[46]

This story echoes Brown Htoo's insistence that the Karen people were the elder and favored son of God long ago. It also explains how the Karen people lost their written language. All of the various Karen groups were preliterate before the arrival of the American missionaries. Still, their rich oral traditions seemingly prophesied the coming of a lost white brother who would one day return to emancipate the Karen people from oppression.

The Story of Htot Meh Pah

The most referenced Karen story Brown and Sam Ber Htoo would recount to me was the story of Htot Meh Pah (also spelled Poo Htot Meh Pah, grandfather boar tusk), the Karen progenitor. Again, Yoko Hayami offers a version that best fits with the story I have pieced together over the years.

> Long ago there were two brothers. The older was Karen and the younger, a white man. They lived near a river in Burma with their Tho Mae Pa (Father

Boar Tusk). Tho Mae Pa had a comb made from a boar's tusk which brought eternal life to its user. Tho Mae Pa and his children therefore enjoyed eternal life and increased in numbers. Their land was getting too crowded, and one day, Tho Mae Pa brought his children to this river to seek new land. The two brothers were hungry. The elder Karen brother cooked mud snails, and the younger white brother, crabs. The hard shells of the mud snails wouldn't soften, and while the elder Karen waited endlessly, the younger finished cooking the crab and ate, and went on ahead with Tho Mae Pa. He and the comb had gone forever, while the Karen was left to himself on this side of the river.[47]

As with the previous story of Ywa, Karen and whites are brothers. Interestingly, in this story, the emphasis is placed on the loss of the white brother and eternal life (the comb made from a boar tusk). This was also the story Brown Htoo was referencing when, early on in my visits to the family, he half-jokingly described my presence in his family's life as a "return of the white brother sent by God." The complete version of the oral poem or *hta* revealing this story is related in Karen General Smith Dun's memoir.

> The Karen was the elder brother,
> And obtained all the words of God,
> God formerly loved the Karen nation above all others,
> But because of their transgressions, he cursed them,
> And now they have no books.
> Yet he will again have mercy on them. And love them above all others
> 'God departed with our younger brother,
> The white foreigner.
> He conducted God away to the West.
> God gave them power to cross waters and reach lands
> And to have rulers among themselves. Then God went up to heaven
> But He made the white foreigners
> More skillful than all other nations.
> 'when God had departed
> 'the Karens became slaves to the Burmans,
> Became sons of the forest and children of poverty;
> Were scattered everywhere.
> The Burmans made them labour bitterly,
> Till many dropped down dead in the jungle,
> Or they twisted their arms behind them,
> Beat them with stripes, and pounded them with the elbow,
> Days without end.[48]

It has never been clear to me what transgressions led to such loss for the Karen people. Yet, this theme of a Karen fall from grace is common in nineteenth-century accounts. What is clearer is that Karen redemption comes with the return of their younger white brother, thus indebting the Karen people to their younger white saviors and ushering in a new era for Karen people. Such stories offered Sgaw Karen Christians like Brown

Htoo some explanation for their historical oppression and justification for Karen conversion.

And the rate of Karen conversion was unparalleled. This spread is even more remarkable when we consider that it occurred across a vast and underdeveloped region with no roads or formal lines of communication. It is no wonder many Karen and missionaries alike continue to believe this conversion rate is divinely inspired. Within the first forty years of the arrival of the Judsons in Burma, the missionaries had translated the Bible into two languages, Burmese and Sgaw Karen, and parts of the Bible were being translated into three additional languages![49] In comparison, after nearly two hundred years of working with Native American tribes, the Bible had only been translated into two Native American languages.[50]

These early American missionaries were divided in their objectives with the Karen people. According to Jay Riley Case, some missionaries took a more "civilizing" approach to transform the Karen into the image of their Western benefactors. In contrast, others saw in the Karen people a chance toward "democratization."[51] Both approaches would leave a legacy on the Sgaw Karen people in particular. Many Sgaw Karen would gain status through their ties with Christian missionaries and later British colonizers. Ideals about democracy and the organizational capacity instilled by the American missionaries may have been another motivation for the Karen to insist on autonomy after independence.

The connections between Karen oral traditions related to a single god, Ywa, certainly helped support the early proselytizing efforts of missionaries. Regardless of the veracity of this or the many other assertions that divinely link the Karen to Christianity and their white brother, the reality is that generations of Karen continue to believe, like Brown Htoo and now his son, Sam Ber Htoo, that the white brother returned God, eternal life through Jesus (salvation), and the written word to the Karen people. However, it is important to recognize that the arrival of the white brother is not the end of the Karen prophecy, as Brown often related to me through his sons.

In the end, the Karen people will become the true kings of the earth. Again, General Smith Dun provides the second part of the *hta* foretelling the rise of a Karen king of kings after their emancipation by their younger white brother.

> In the midst of their sufferings
> They [the Karen people] remembered the ancient sayings of the elders,
> That God would yet save them,
> That a Karen king would yet appear.
> The Talien kings have had their season;
> The Siamese kings have had their season;
> And the foreign kings will have their season;

But the Karen king will yet appear.
When he arrives, there will be but one monarch
And there will be neither rich nor poor
Everything will be happy,
And even lions and leopards will lose their savageness.
"Hence in their deep afflictions they prayed,
If God will save us,
Let him save speedily!
We can endure these sufferings no longer.
Alas! Where is God?
Our ancestors said that when our younger brothers came back,
The white foreigners
Who were able to keep company with God,
Everything will be happy."[52]

Interestingly, the white brother's return not only emancipates the Karen people from centuries of oppression but paves the way toward the fulfillment of Ywa's grand plan to make the Karen the kings of kings. I think this is an important aspect of the Karen story that is often overlooked when we consider the discourse surrounding the Karen as victims and refugees.

The Karen people have long been depicted as victims, yet the story is complex. Many within the Sgaw Karen leadership view their oppression as only a step toward their inevitable return to power. They do not see themselves as simple victims of oppression and struggle but, rather, the chosen ones who will one day rule. While this may be part of the propaganda perpetuated by Christian Sgaw leaders, it has served the Christian Sgaw Karen leadership.

The Karen national anthem was written in 1900 by Thra San Ba, a Karen Christian who studied at Andover Newton Theological School.[53] It reiterates the message that the Karen are destined for greatness.

Oh, daw ka lu of mine, the best people abide, I love you the best, you value honesty, and hospitality, all noble qualities, I love you most The Lord's chosen children, the folks expecting God, blessed you are, you'd been persecuted, though been enslaved as well, white brother liberators, God sent them back, The God of our fathers, our hope from olden days, we worship thee, to be thy disciples, carry gospel message, to very [every] sea and land, bless us oh lord.[54]

This story is even more salient when considering that the narrative persists today. Brown Htoo and other Karen elders view resettlement to the United States as another step toward fulfilling this divine plan of setting the Karen back in their rightful place as God's favored people. Interestingly, when I pressed Brown Htoo on what was meant by "kings of the world," he was less specific but indicated that the Karen people would be kings of Thailand and Burma. But what I find most interesting is how this story demonstrates the independence and pride of the Karen people.

During my ten years with the Karen community in Sandville and other Karen communities in the United States, most whites involved with the Karen were Christian preachers or volunteers from a Christian-based organization. I was one of the few whites who worked with Karen populations not affiliated with a religious group. Today, various Christian denominations and other religions actively pursue Karen families, namely the Church of Latter-Day Saints and the Jehovah's Witness.

Brown often asked me why I was not speaking of Jesus more with his sons. I tried to explain to him through one of his sons that my book of wisdom was secular and that I was focused on helping his children learn English so that they might have more opportunities. He accepted this begrudgingly. As I think back, I believe Brown viewed the growing secularism of the United States as another sign of the fulfillment of that ancient prophecy that foretold the return of the Karen people to their former status as favored daughters and sons of Ywa. And in some ways, elders like Brown view some of their white brothers (Americans) as squandering their preferred status through a loss of faith. And to my complete dismay, many Karen elders in Sandville and around the United States considered Donald Trump to be "sent by God" to right the ship in the United States.

The fact remains that American missionaries capitalized on these Karen prophecies and made sure to put them in print at the earliest opportunity to fulfill the return of the Karen book of knowledge, the King James Bible. Creating a Karen orthography (Karen script) provided a translation of the Sgaw Karen Bible, now available on Google Play!

Today, most of the literature reports that the majority of Sgaw Karen are Christian. What is less than certain is what percentage of all Karen are Christian. We know that Karen Christians, namely Baptist or Seventh Day Adventists have held positions of power.[55] According to the US government, which documents religious and ethnic affiliation, Karen Christians make up nearly 70 percent of all Karen resettled to the United States.[56] For me, this number seems an underestimate and, at the very least, does not account for those who have converted since arriving.

The reality is that Christianity has had a major influence on Sgaw Karen families like the Htoos, whose ancestors are claimed to be among the first Christian converts.

Early Western Depictions of the Karen

The views of the missionaries and British colonial officers working with the Karen in the early days also set a precedent on how the Karen would be represented over the next two hundred years and deserve some attention. A troubling but common portrayal of the Karen in nineteenth-

century US and British colonial accounts presents the Karen in two seemingly contradictory terms: shy and savage. One of the first Western missionary accounts of the Karen comes from Mrs. Judson soon after making
contact with the Karen and is typical of early portrayals. She writes: "The
Karens are a meek, peaceful, simple and credulous race with many of the
softer virtues and few flagrant vices. Though greatly addicted to drunk-
enness, extremely filthy, and indolent in their habits, their morals in other
respects are superior to many more civilized races."[57]

Later accounts like those of V.W. Wallace (British Commissioner of the
Irrawaddy Division) offer another common depiction of Karen aloofness.

> The fact is the Karens are a shy race, suffering from a sort of desire to keep
> aloof from all other people, and seldom showing any wish to interview of-
> ficials unless they have proved their friendliness by learning their language
> and customs and moving amongst them. Even then, to many persons, the
> Karen may appear to be surly and ungrateful, but this is only due to his nat-
> ural shyness and the repression of all outward signs of his feelings.[58]

Similar accounts of the Karen people are found today. I had the opportunity to talk with one middle-aged American neighbor of a Karen family
in Milwaukee, Wisconsin, whose description could have come from those
early portrayals.

> They are nice, yes. But they are all so shy. We're a friendly family, always
> were really and try to be neighborly. The mother, or at least I think she is, the
> tiny one there with baby, I don't think she's ever raised her eyes above my
> knees. The kids will talk with me all right. They'll come right into the house.
> But the parents, not a word in over two years. Just nervous-like smiles.[59]

I will not forget one occasion when I pulled my car up the driveway of a
Karen family new to the area and unfamiliar with my car or me. They all
scampered into their house as I approached and peeked out the windows
as I parked. They did not come out until one of my Karen students got out
of the car.

The shyness of the Karen people is found in nearly every nineteenth-
century account. As Brown Htoo would often tell me, such wariness of
strangers has helped the Karen survive and maintain their unique cultural identity. Such reticence is also a byproduct of their historical sub-
jugation by the majority Burmans and their more recent displacement
from their native villages, their flight into Thailand, and their prolonged
stay in refugee camps. Staying under the radar was a means of survival
as they fled Burma and sought sanctuary in Thailand. And that same
caution and weariness of Thai authorities helped them survive the many
years in refugee camps where many often ventured beyond the camp's
fences to work on Thai farms or seek other employment. However, this

penchant for shyness and staying out of the way has dire consequences in the United States.

Sam Ber Htoo often related to me disturbing reports of Karen not reporting crimes perpetrated against them in urban areas. According to Sam Ber Htoo, their fear of the police and coming out of the shadows preclude reports of rape, theft, and other crimes that often go unreported by Karen in the United States. In rural Sandville, they felt more able to handle things internally. Karen shyness has direct implications for teaching and learning, as discussed in chapters 4 and 5. Regarding education, Karen students and families will often forgo asking for help or asking questions due to their deferential attitude toward those in authority. Their "shyness" can also prevent them from having a voice in their child's education.

Christianity, Language, Education, and Karen Identity

Like other later nineteenth-century missionary efforts in Africa, the South Pacific, and Asia, American Christian missionaries introduced written language to the Sgaw and other Karen groups. The illusion that the Karen were a homogeneous Christian group created a pan-Karen identity. Later, missionaries devised competing orthographies for various Karen dialects and other Christianized ethnic groups like the Chin and Karenni with the same result. Pwo Karen have a Thai-based orthography, and the Karenni and Chin have a romanized script. But the Sgaw Karen have a writing system based on Burmese characters.

The missionaries made literacy a major goal of their proselytizing enterprise. As James Lee Lewis contends, "writing down the language was the primal effort in the evangelization of the Karens."[60] In addition to translating the Bible, the missionaries established a very active printing press, which allowed for the mass dissemination of mostly Christian texts, school primers, traditional folktales in the form of *htas* (oral poems), and Sgaw Karen newspapers.[61] The missionaries' establishment of a Karen printing press enabled Western and later Sgaw Karen missionaries to spread the gospel while propagating a new Christian identity.[62]

Importantly, the introduction of a Sgaw Karen script provided many Karen literacy and enhanced the divide between Karens and Burmans. And language became another target of Karen oppression. As Dun reports in his memoir: "if any Karen in Burmese territory was found to have learned the art of reading and writing, the penalty was death by crucifixion."[63] Though literacy further polarized Karen-Burman relations, literacy provided the Karen people with more social, economic, and cultural capital. Brown Htoo often spoke of his pride in a written script uniquely Karen.

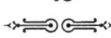

The first Sgaw Karen newspaper was first published in the mid-nineteenth century. The *Morning Star Today* became "a mouthpiece for Christian ideas."[64] According to Charles F. Keyes:

> The missionaries initiated the development of a Karen literate tradition, beginning with translating the Bible into Karen and including the publication of folklore supportive of Christian ideas from a very early time. The construction of printing presses to serve both religious and educational needs also stimulated the emergence of a Karen press and a tradition of secular literature. The Karen Christian churches (mainly Baptist) have provided a network of connections and an organization that is more than local. Missionaries have also attracted support from non-Karen circles in Burma, India, England, and the United States.[65]

Today, cell phones, digital video (pirated DVDs), social networking sites, and other Karen-made websites have become the primary means of disseminating Karen religious, secular, and nationalist ideas.[66] Christian publications continue to serve Karen communities in Burma, the refugee camps, and diaspora communities across the United States, connecting resettled Karen from Brisbane to Boston. I observed Brown Htoo and other Karen elders reading *Go Forward*, a Karen Baptist Convention (KBC) publication out of Rangoon, Burma.

Sgaw Karen communities across the United States try to maintain the Sgaw Karen language. Sandville had a very active summer program for Sgaw Karen language, music, and Bible study that is helping the community maintain its heritage, culture, language, and religion. These courses were always a favorite of mine to observe because I was able to witness how these children were being educated "Karen-style." Based on the brothers' description of the harsh disciplinary education in the camps, I was surprised to see a more lax and communicative teaching style for older children.

And many of the traditional education practices established by those early missionaries continue post-resettlement in communities like Sandville. At the end of each Karen summer school session, students of all age levels have a recitation competition often judged by elders in the community or other visiting dignitaries from other US communities, Burma, or Thailand. Children are judged on accuracy, the harmony of speech, and Karen attire. Winners receive a cash prize. Such events are another way the community can maintain Sgaw Karen culture, language, and religion. Importantly, these types of schooling experiences reinforce Karen educational practices, which tend to favor teacher-centered learning and might be why some Karen children remain quiet and passive in US classrooms.

Like most refugees, Brown and Esther considered their children's education a primary motivation for their flight from Burma and eventual resettlement in the United States. This emphasis on education dates back to the establishment of mission schools, which aimed to spread the gospel by teaching the Karen people to read and write. Brown's maternal grandparents were among those Karen families who directly benefited from a mission education, and both went on to work at mission schools. Other Karen could use their new literacy to hold positions within the British colonial enterprise. San C. Po writes, "the Karens recognized an association between literacy and power, and the missionaries' emphasis on imparting literacy skills served as an important draw to Karens determined to improve their status."[67] Later, Karens would use their literacy to disseminate nationalist literature and help establish a Karen identity.

Today, many in Sandville and throughout the Karen diaspora support in principle the continued efforts of the Karen National Liberation Army (KNLA) and its political wing, the KNU. The church-military resistance alliance is evident with renewed fighting in Burma since February 2021 and yet another military crackdown. Lewis summarizes it best when he writes, "The writing down again of the Karen language, while a marvel to the Karens themselves, raised them in their own estimation and gave them a new status among the people of Burma . . . the Karen were raised in official status from 'depressed causes' to one of the 'civilized races.'"[68]

The Legacy of Animism

It is also important to recognize that despite the importance of Christianity on Sgaw Karen culture and identity over the past two hundred years, most Karen groups were originally Animist. Today, many Pwo Karen (the second largest Karen group) are Buddhist or Buddhist-Animist, and some Sgaw Karen are Animist. Interestingly, despite their strong association with Christianity, many Karen like Brown and Esther have maintained many Animist beliefs to interpret the world around them. These stories were always a fascination of the Htoo brothers and mine and are presented in subsequent chapters. It is also important to note that conversion to Christianity continues post-resettlement. As one Karen Buddhist living in North Carolina told me, "It is tough to be Buddhist Karen in the US as there are so few of us and people convert because they want to be members of the Karen community and have resources."

The British-Karen Alliance

In addition to American missionary benefactors, British expansion east from India led to three Anglo-Burmese wars pitting the Anglo-Indian Army, with the support of the Karen, against the Kingdom of Arakon. If the missionaries brought spiritual and linguistic salvation to the Karen, the British offered more material and economic aid and security. Under the British, the Karen found an ally and protector and an asset that would provide new status, safety, and educational advancement throughout the colonial era. For many analysts and scholars,[69] this relationship between the British colonial enterprise and the Karen missionary-alignment created Karen identity and later nationalistic aspirations.

Many Karen served the British as guides during the First Anglo-Burmese War in 1825 and then as active military personnel. They aided the British in their military efforts against the Burmese in the second and third Anglo-Burmese wars, joined the British in World War I, and later fought alongside the British against the Japanese during World War II.[70] Under the British, the Karen came to dominate the armed forces.[71]

The Karen had a disproportionate representation in the Burmese Army. As late as 1939 (ten years before independence), the Karen had 1,448 troops compared to only 472 Burmans serving in the Burmese Army.[72] Karen General Smith Dun acted as the first commander-in-chief of independent Burma but was quickly replaced because of the Karen insurgency.[73]

The Education of the Karen

If language was the primary goal of the missionaries (i.e., creating a Karen written language), education was a goal of both missionaries and the British colonial enterprise. The British and missionary enterprises established the first organized network of schools for the Karen and promoted Karen literacy in both Sgaw Karen and English. Some earnest Karen students won scholarships to England and the United States for postsecondary education. Many American and British educated Karen became teachers, nurses, policemen, soldiers and held other civil servant positions during the colonial period.

Many of the earliest nationalist leaders and thinkers, such as Saw Baw Oo Gyi and Sir San Crombie Po, were educated in Great Britain and the United States. Karen intellectual Sir San Crombie Po arrived in the United States for his studies when he was fourteen years old and studied to be a medical doctor. He became a vocal supporter of British rule and represented the attitude of many westernized Karen toward British and US patrons. He writes, "The Karens are not ashamed or afraid to proclaim to the world publicly or in private that they owe what progress and advancement they have made, to the missionaries whom they affectionately call their 'Mother,' under the protection of the British who they rightly call their 'Father.'"[74]

Table 1.1. Nineteenth-Century Karen History. © Daniel Gilhooly.

Year	Event
1813	Arrival of American Baptist Missionaries Adoniram and Ann Judson in the Kingdom of Ava
1824–26	First of the three Anglo-Burmese Wars
1829	Ko Tha Byu is the first Karen convert to Christianity
1832	Christian missionaries acquire first printing press
1842	Sgaw Karen language newspaper, *The Morning Star*, is established
1845	The establishment of the Karen Baptist Theological Seminary
1853	The start of the Second Anglo-Burmese War The first Sgaw Karen Bible is published
1858	Bucknell University hosts the first Karen university student
1865	The founding of the Burma Baptist Convention
1881	The establishment of the Karen National Association (KNA)
1885	Final Annexation of Burma by the British in the Third Anglo-Burmese War

This paternalistic attitude toward the West has come to dominate Western discourse related to the Karen ever since, namely because these westernized leaders had the advantage of Western education and an English voice in print, from the pulpit, and later politically. And their ties to American missionaries have persevered until today.

The Karen also benefited from their relocation from the hills to the Delta, where they were provided land to farm to support the British rice industry.[75] The fertile soils of the Irrawaddy Delta offered arable lands and the safety of a region with long missionary and colonial development.[76] However, these advantages came with a price post-independence as those Karen who most benefited lost their favored status upon British withdrawal.

In short, British involvement in Burma left a mark on the nation and many Karen people, but the most lasting impact the British may have had was in creating a Karen identity in the first place. British efforts to categorize all the ethnic groups in many ways created the various ethnic identities that now, and in the past, merged under ethnic banners. As Kwanchewan Buadaeng contends: "the formation of ethnic consciousness and identities began only after ethnic classification by the British."[77] When we add to this the privileged status the Karen experienced under the protection of Western missionaries, it is no wonder that tension with the Burmese escalated. A civil war broke out soon after independence.

As Table 1.1 illustrates, nineteenth-century Karen history is marked by colonial and missionary enterprises. The table also illustrates how quickly the American missionary enterprise was able to help develop Karen Christianity, literacy (i.e., printing press), US-Karen relations (i.e., Karen students in the United States), and nationalist aspirations (i.e., the establishment of nationalist groups like the KNU).

Literacy, white men and women (Americans and British), nationalism, Karen ethnic identity, and Christianity are all entangled for Christian Sgaw Karen like the Htoos. I leave it to my reader to consider the full scope of the epistemological and ontological implications Christianity has had on the Karen people, as it is beyond the scope of this book. What is clear is that Sgaw Karen culture traditions are alive and well as is evident in the Htoo's rural community of Sandville, Georgia.

Notes

Epigraph: Smeaton, *Loyal Karens*, 63.

1. McMahon, *Karens Golden Chersonese*, 46.
2. McMahon, *Karens Golden Chersonese*, 46.
3. Cady, *History Modern Burma* as quoted in Hayami, "Between Hills and Plains," 36.
4. Buadaeng, *Ethnic Identities Karen*, 88.
5. Buadaeng, *Ethnic Identities Karen*, 88–89.
6. Buadaeng, *Ethnic Identities Karen*, 73.
7. Saw MoeTroo and Mika Rolley. n.d.: 1, as quoted in Rajah, *Remaining Karen*, 251.

8. Saw MoeTroo and Mika Rolley. n.d.: 1, as quoted in Rajah, *Remaining Karen,* 251.
9. Moonieinda, *Karen People, 5.*
10. Cusano, "Burma: Displaced Karens," 140.
11. Cusano, "Burma: Displaced Karens," 143.
12. Nieman et al., "Karen."
13. Dun, *Memoirs,* 1.
14. Marshall, *Karen People,* 116.
15. Approximately 72,322 are Karen out of a total 179,869 Burmese as of August 2019.
16. WRAPS, *Refugee Processing Center.*
17. Gilhooly and Lee, "Rethinking Refugee Resettlement," 10.
18. Cusano, "Burma: Displaced Karens," 142.
19. Falla, *True Love and Bartholomew,* 129.
20. Marshall, *Karen People.*
21. Smeaton, *Loyal Karens,* 158.
22. Ott, *Get Up and Go.*
23. Hein, "Refugees, Immigrants."
24. McMahon, *Karens Golden Chersonese,* 52.
25. Case, *Unpredictable Gospel,* 19.
26. Gilhooly and Lee, "Rethinking Refugee Resettlement."
27. McBrien, "Educational Needs and Barriers," 333.
28. Barron et al., *Refugees from Burma,* 35.
29. Marshall, *Karen People,* 128.
30. Marshall, *Karen People,* 129.
31. Barron et al., *Refugees from Burma,* 32.
32. Marshall, *Karen People,* 129.
33. Marshall, *Karen People,* 130.
34. Oh and Van Der Stouwe, "Education, Diversity, Inclusion", 61.
35. Ferrars and Ferrars, *Burma,* 128.
36. Interview, Sam Ber Htoo, 6 June 2010.
37. Marshall, *Karen People,* 29.
38. Lewis, "Burmanization of the Karen," 84.
39. de Jong, "Nineteenth-Century New England Exegete," 319.
40. Case, *Unpredictable Gospel,* 23.
41. Mason, *Karen Apostle Ko Thah-Byu,* 13.
42. Smeaton, *Loyal Karens,* 185.
43. Smeaton *Loyal Karens,* 185.
44. McMahon, *Karens Golden Chersonese,* 194–195.
45. Ywa is the Karen word for God.
46. Hayami, "Karen Tradition," 338.
47. Hayami, "Karen Tradition," 338.
48. Dun, *Memoirs,* 6-7.
49. Case, *Unpredictable Gospel,* 34.
50. Case, *Unpredictable Gospel,* 34.
51. Case, *Unpredictable Gospel,* 36.

52. Dun, *Memoirs*, 6.
53. Thawnghmung, *The "Other" Karen*, 30.
54. Petry, "Sword of the Spirit," 125 as quoted in Thawnghmung, *The "Other" Karen*, 30.
55. South, "Karen Nationalist Communities," 60.
56. WRAPS, *Refugee Processing Center.*
57. Mrs. Judson as quoted McMahon, *Karens Golden Chersonese*, 50.
58. As quoted in Po, *Burma and the Karens*, 35.
59. Interview transcript, neighbor of Karen family, 29 June 2011.
60. Lewis, "Burmanization of the Karen," 204.
61. Lewis, "Burmanization of the Karen," 126.
62. Gravers, *Exploring Ethnic Diversity*, 228.
63. Dun, *Memoirs,* 65.
64. Harriden, "Making a Name for Themselves," 96–97.
65. Keyes, *Golden Peninsula*, 96.
66. Gilhooly and Lee, "Role of Digital Literacy," 7.
67. Po, *Burma and the Karens*, xii.
68. Lewis, "Burmanization of the Karen," 83.
69. See Buadaeng, *Ethnic Identities*; Cheesman, "'Seeing' Karen"; Glesne, *Becoming Qualitative Researchers*; Harriden "Making a Name for Themselves"; South, "Karen Nationalist Communities," *Burma's Longest War*; Thawnghmung, *Karen Revolution in Burma.*
70. Buadaeng, *Ethnic Identities*, 87.
71. Smith, *Burma: Insurgency*, 44.
72. Smith, *Burma: Insurgency*, 44.
73. Dun, *Memoirs.*
74. Po, *Burma and the Karens*, 58.
75. Charney, *History of Modern Burma*, 21.
76. Lewis, "Burmanization of the Karen," 35–36.
77. Buadaeng, *Ethnic Identities*, 75.

Chapter 2

The Htoos

The Road from Burma
to the United States

Sleep together, be warm; eat together, the food is delicious.
—Karen proverb

The life stories of Brown Htoo and Esther Htoo represent two of the many Karen diaspora stories. The family's flight from Burma, protracted stay in refugee camps in Thailand, their subsequent decision to apply for resettlement, and their eventual resettlement to the United States have forever changed the course of their, their children, and now their grandchildren's lives. Each of those decisions—to flee, to wait, and to apply—were all forced upon them by historical forces that caught them in the maelstrom that was post-colonial Burma.

Like many refugee parents who apply for resettlement to third countries like the United States, the decision is selfless. Brown and Esther's decision was predicated on believing that their children would have better futures in the United States. It was and is still unclear to me what that vision of a "better" life was or what it has become, but I sometimes wonder if they might ever regret the decision they made a decade ago (this will be addressed later in the epilogue). I imagine they still must long for their native villages and wake from dreams that take them back to their native land. But I think they both know there is no going back, and they are resigned to what God has ordained. Whenever I go down this mental path I think of my last picture of Brown standing proudly holding his US naturalization certificate with pride and not a hint of regret (see figure 3.1).

Figure 2.1. Brown Htoo and Esther (2012). © Daniel Gilhooly

I believe he and Esther had little idea about the ramifications of moving to the United States before their compulsory three-day language and
culture-training course offered by the International Organization for Migration (IOM). This wholly insufficient preparation course was provided
only a few days before boarding a plane bound for the United States.
They had seen movies. But how do the Rambo franchise and *Braveheart*
(the Htoo brothers' favorite films at the time) prepare you for life in urban
America?

By 2006, when they initially applied with the United Nations High
Commissioner for Refugees (UNHCR) for resettlement, they had lived in
three camps for nearly seventeen years. The prospects of staying or poten-
tially returning to Burma were equally grim. Despite reforms and seeming
steps toward democratization and peace, a return to Burma was viewed
with suspicion and uncertainty. There was no way for them to trust the
Burmese generals, and they were left with two options: stay in the camps
indefinitely or register to resettle.

The younger generation, sons and nephews, encouraged Brown and
Esther to register for resettlement. After nearly two decades in the camps,
they had established roots, not deep roots but roots nonetheless. They had

always thought they would return to their native Burma, but after seventeen years of confinement and uncertainty, it was time to go, and for the first time, they had options. After consulting with their extended family, they decided to apply for resettlement in 2016.

Brown's nephew was the first to leave Mae La for Norway in 2016, and his phone calls on life in Norway offered the Htoos a sense of the realities and opportunities that awaited them. Yet, the Htoo family was among the first to resettle, and the resettlement program in Norway is far different than what the Htoos would face in the United States. In many ways, families like the Htoos were the guinea pigs, and the hard lessons they learned would be shared with subsequent resettlers.[1] The term "resettlers" was borrowed from Rebekah Brown who describes resettlers as "shorthand for the multivalent experiences and actions of the first and second generations of refugee-background migrants."[2] I like the term as it seems to give some agency to those who make the decision to apply for resettlement and then do it.

The Htoos are part of a much larger Karen and Burmese diaspora story that has seen the departure of Karen people to communities across Australia, Norway, Canada, the United Kingdom, and the United States. Like most Karen refugees arriving in the United States, Brown and Esther's story begins in their native villages in Burma.

Brown and Esther: Burmese Days

Brown Htoo (Brown Gold) was born in 1953 in the Irrawaddy Delta of lower Burma in the town of Myaungmya, Irrawaddy Region, south of Pathein (Bassein), one of the strongholds of the American missionaries. His family lived alongside Buddhist Karen and ethnic Burmans.

His family represents the Karen families whom the British relocated to the Irrawaddy Delta region to increase rice production in the nineteenth century. Myaungmya became synonymous with Karen-Burmese violence during the Japanese occupation of Burma. The massacre of Karen villagers at the hands of the Burmese Independence Army (BIA) "loomed very large in the collective memory of Karen and changed forever their place in the Burmese community."[3] Myaungmya, like other areas of the Irrawaddy Delta with Karen populations, saw communal riots and the massacre of many Karen, which was a prelude to the violence that would spread after independence.

His name "Brown" is an Anglo-Karen name. He told me via his son Hser Ku Htoo that he was named Brown because of his dark complexion. When asked why he was given the English name Brown rather than the

Sgaw Karen word for "brown," he told me of his grandmother's fluency in English. Like elsewhere, English is a sign of status for the Karen, which may be why he was given the English name Brown.[4]

Brown's maternal grandparents, Nelly and Aung Pyu, worked at a missionary school in Myaungmya. She was a teacher, and her husband became a Karen Baptist mission school principal. However, due to the growing hostilities between the Karen and the Burmese government and some of their neighbors, most of Brown's generation would not be afforded the same education as their parents. The loss of English instruction was one casualty. Brown had only brief exposure to English schooling in his youth and still has very limited speaking proficiency in English. Yet, he often proudly touted his parents' command of English.

Brown Htoo had three siblings: one sister, Naw Ma Gray, recently died in Burma, and the other sister, Htoo Htoo (Gold Gold), resides nearby in Sandville. Htoo Htoo was one of the first Karen I met in the area, and she was always eager to share her experiences with me. Brown's brother, Po Say, was killed in Burma—his killing was unrelated to ethnic tensions or the civil war, but he was killed at the hands of a Burman during a robbery. Maybe this added to Brown's inability to trust the Burmese government.

Like most Karen from the Delta, his ancestors farmed rice and lived peaceably side by side with ethnic Burmans. Brown Htoo grew up speaking his native Sgaw Karen at home and the language of his neighbors, Burmese, in school. By the time he was born in 1953, much had changed for his family, the nascent nation of Burma (only in existence for five years at the time), and the Karen people.

Independence and the Insurgency: Sixty Years of Civil War

For the Karen people, foreboding about their fate after independence and the withdrawal of their British benefactors began during the Japanese occupation of Burma during World War II. According to Karen writer Spencer Zan,[5] the BIA was responsible for the massacre of many Karen during the Japanese occupation of Burma during World War II. Karen insurgency groups began to form in response to these attacks on Karen villages. Much of the inner-ethnic violence occurred in the Delta regions of Burma in Brown's hometown of Myaungmya, but Brown's family had escaped persecution. It is also important to remember that many Karen were soldiers under the British. This training in warfare and the availability of weapons and their organizational capacity made the Karen insurrection particularly effective after independence.

Independence from Great Britain was far from a seamless or peaceful transition and left in its wake political turmoil that continues until today. In the run-up to independence, Aung Sahn, father of pro-democracy leader and Nobel Peace Prize winner Aung San Suu Kyi, was assassinated. With his death came the end of hope for multiethnic coalition rule. For educated Karen like San C. Po, Aung San had been able to "win a degree of trust amongst many Karen."[6] The Karen people, along with other ethnic minorities and communist groups, began fighting the government soon after independence. For those Karen who took up arms, the goal was an independent Karen State.

However, like most Karen, Brown Htoo's family did not take up arms and, though they supported the insurgency in principle, stayed out of the fight. Before reading Ardeth Thawnghmung's insightful book *The "Other" Karen in Myanmar: Ethnic Minorities and the Struggle without Arms*,[7] I had assumed that most Karen were actively involved in the fighting. In fact, in the early days with the Karen families in Sandville, DVDs capturing the ongoing "fight" were often shown to me. It was clear that the fighting was continuing and that the fighting was of interest to parents and Karen elders. But most Karen were not actively engaged in the fighting.

Thawnghmung demystifies the narrative that all Karens were active participants in the fight, as many Karen leaders profess. When I addressed this with Brown Htoo, he reluctantly agreed but indicated that all Karen supported the efforts of the insurgency. In short, most Karen were like Brown's family who never actively fought. Though not involved directly in the insurgency, many of Brown's generation were and still remain very nationalistic and adhere to the four principles established by their founding leader, Saw Ba Oo Gyi.

1. Surrender is out of the question.
2. The recognition of the Karen State must be completed.
3. We shall retain our arms.
4. We shall decide our own political destiny.[8]

Saw Ba Oo Gyi, the first president of the Karen National Union, still maintains a strong presence within the diaspora, including within the Htoo family. According to Sang Kook Lee, every Karen home in Mae La Camps has an image of Saw Ba Oo Gyi and his four principles.[9] Like many young Karen too young to have even experienced the fight, Sam Ber Htoo often sported a t-shirt with the image of Saw Ba Oo Gyi on the front and his four principles on the back.

His image adorns t-shirts, banners, living room walls, calendars, and bumper stickers across the United States. During the annual Karen Martyr's Day celebration each 12 August, Karen communities across the diaspora commemorate the death of Saw Ba Oo Gyi. Interestingly, starting in

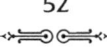

2019, various Karen organizations in the United States descend on Washington, DC, each 12 August to denounce the regime in Burma and call for increased measures by the US government to hold the generals accountable. It is important to note that Sa Ba Oo Gyi was Western-educated and Christian.

By the time Brown Htoo was ten years old in 1963, the country was experiencing multiple insurgencies throughout the nation. General Ne Win's military coup in 1962 began an era of military rule in Burma that continues until today. However, for much of the first four decades after independence, the Karen, though not officially, had control of much of the Karen State (known officially as the Kayin State). They had created a de facto government and infrastructure replete with schools, hospitals, a tax system, trade organizations, forestry service, an executive branch, army, judiciary, prison system, as well as an active church network.[10]

The KNU and its military wing, KNLA, ruled the Karen State with relative autonomy until the late 1980s. This state, known to the Karen as Kawthoohlei (literally a "land without darkness"), functioned with relative autonomy from the government in Rangoon and was financially stable due to illegal trade with Thailand controlled by the KNU.[11] Kawthoohlei was also where Brown's future wife Esther was born.[12]

Esther

Esther was born in the village of Kawkareik, Karen State, less than 50 km from the Thai border but 550 km from her future husband. Like her husband, Esther was Baptist Christian, yet she was brought up within a black zone, or free-fire zone, where villagers spotted outside designated areas could be shot without warning.[13] By the late 1970s, the Tatmadaw (Burmese Armed Forces) had eliminated many of their former foes, but the KNU stubbornly resisted and held onto many areas within Kawthoolei. The stubborn resistance of the KNU and other ethnic and political insurgency groups only heightened Ne Win's oppression. The junta under Ne Win aimed to eliminate the four elements sustaining the insurgency: food, funds, recruits, and information.[14] This campaign began by dividing the country into zones: black (insurgent-controlled), brown (contested areas) and white zones (government-controlled).

Amid this turmoil, Esther attended school until age sixteen, an unusually high level of education for her generation. After finishing school, she continued to help her parents plant and harvest rice and care for her younger siblings. Esther watched as her brother left to join the KNLA as a child of twelve, and experienced firsthand the terror of Ne Win's Four

Cuts. She also watched as another brother traveled from village to village collecting "taxes" to help fund the insurgency.

Meanwhile, Brown watched as childhood friends left the Delta to join the resistance movement or flee to the safety of the Thai-Burmese border. Brown stayed and worked with his father, attended school, and studied the Bible. By his late teens, he studied at a Bible school and trained to become a missionary under Pastor Wah Doh (White Uncle). In his late twenties, Brown left home and headed for the dwindling black zones of the Karen State to preach the gospel. Unlike some of his peers, he left the Delta with a Bible instead of a gun.

For over five years, he traveled among the villages of the many hill tribes of the Karen State. He lived off the land and hunted and fished for his sustenance. Brown relied on the generosity of villagers for a roof to sleep under and food when he was unable to provide for himself. He preached in his native Sgaw Karen, Pwo Karen, and Burmese to villagers who spoke one of twelve mutually unintelligible Karen dialects. Although he worked mainly with Sgaw villages, he preached to Pwo and Bgu Karen villagers. He was committed to saving the souls of his Animist, Muslim, and Buddhist brothers and sisters alike.

In 1983, after nearly five years of mission work, he arrived in the town of Kawkareik, where he met Esther. He was introduced to her as a possible match. Brown hoped to marry Esther, but because he was always on the move and needed permission from the mission society to settle down, he could not stay in Kawkareik. He promised to return, and after seven months away, he kept his word. They were married the following day.

They remained in Kawkareik, where both helped with farming and where Brown occasionally preached. Two years later, in 1985, they had a daughter, Sar Ah (after the biblical Sarah, wife of Abraham), and later a son, Moe Tha Wah (Life Heart White). Moe Tha Wah was born amid the near collapse of the Karen State in the now infamous year 1988.

As noted in the introduction, 1988 lives forever in the collective memory of all those Burmese who lived through the brutal crackdown on peaceful demonstrations. The results of the military's bloody crackdown of the multiethnic student protestors led to the flight of student organizers of the protests and a host of ethnic minorities like the Karen. After this chaos, Brown and a pregnant Esther (pregnant with their third child Sam Ber Htoo) decided to leave Burma, hoping for safety in Thailand.

They and their two children boarded a bus that took them within a day's walk of the border with neighboring Thailand that was swelling with displaced Karen and other ethnic minorities. In 1989, they crossed into Thailand amid chaos and uncertainty to start anew.

Table 2.1. The Htoo family and modern Burmese historical events. © Daniel Gilhooly

Burmese History after Independence	The Htoo Family
1948 Burmese Independence **1954** Karen state of Kawthoolei established	**1953** Brown Htoo born in Myaung-mya, Ayeyarwady Region, Burma
1960 Buddhism named state religion of Burma **1962** Ne Win rise to power via military coup, established of Four Cuts policy to eradicate insurgency groups and end "civil war"	**1962** Esther born in Kawkareik, Karen State **1983** Brown Htoo and Esther marry **1986** Sa Rah (daughter) born in Burma
1988 Violent suppression of student protests by Burmese the Tatmadaw	**1988** Moe Tha Wah (son) born in Burma
1989 The country's name is officially changed from Burma to Republic of the Union of Myanmar	**1989** Family flees Burma into Thailand
	1990 Samber Htoo born in Bornho Refugee Camp
	1991 family relocates to Tha Lah Taw Refugee Camp, Thailand
	1992 Hser Gay Htoo born in Tha Lah Taw Refugee Camp, Thailand
	1994 Family relocates to Mae La Refugee Camp, Thailand **1995** Hse Ku Htoo born Mae La Refugee Camp, Thailand **1999** Family officially registered as "refugees"
2006 Bush administration allows for "Burmese" resettlement to USA from camps in Thailand.	**2006** Htoo family applies for resettlement
	2007 Family leaves Mae La Camp for Phoenix Arizona

	2009 Family relocates to Georgia
2012 Karen Burmese government sign Peace Treaty	**2012** Hser Gay Htoo first in family to graduate high school. Family relocates to Iowa
2014 US halts refugee resettlement program from Thai Camps	

Thailand and the Road to Resettlement

The Htoos are what Egon Kunz refers to as anticipatory refugees[15] as they fled Burma due to the threat of violence rather than any direct violence perpetrated upon them. They are among those lucky enough to have avoided direct contact with the Tatmadaw although Brown once told about being forced to porter heavy loads.

Many Karen arriving in Thailand are less lucky. Many arrived traumatized by violence. The atrocities committed by the Tatmadaw, the Democratic Karen Baptist Army (DKBA), and the various ethnic minority insurgency groups have been well documented by Karen and other ethnic minority groups and the international community. Kevin Malseed[16] offers a comprehensive analysis of the human rights violations perpetrated by the Tatmadaw, but many ethnic insurgency groups have also come under scrutiny.

Kevin Heppner's report for Human Rights Watch documents the active recruitment of child soldiers by the Tatmadaw as well as various ethnic groups like the KNLA.[17] Although his report acknowledges efforts by the KNU to stop the recruitment of child soldiers, it is less certain how well these new rules are impacting the realities in the field. The KNU has become very savvy in using digital forums to help control the narrative of their struggle, and evidence suggests that Karen have also been complicit in human rights violations.

As noted earlier, the Karen community in Sandville consumes videos coming out of Burma documenting the guerrilla attacks of the KNLA and the atrocities of the Tatmadaw. Today, many use Facebook to watch in real time the renewed fighting that began as a result of the latest military coup in February 2021. I have watched many of these crude videos documenting the efforts of Karen guerrillas, and it is clear to me that all sides are violating human rights. However, the Tatmadaw list of atrocities is harrowing.

Most ethnic minorities, like the Karen, are forced to porter heavy equipment for the Tatmadaw like Brown described in one of our talks. Others experience rape, torture, the murder of family members, and the burning of villages. Every Karen family I have spoken with about the insurgency has stories about what they or their family and friends experienced in Burma before and during their flight.

Brown and Esther decided that the country was too unstable for them to remain and followed in the footsteps of so many ethnic minorities who had been fleeing to Thailand since the late 1960s. Autobiographical accounts of Karen, such as Spencer Zan's account, offer compelling insights into how long Karen families have been fleeing Burma.

Thailand: The Early Days

Making it safely into Thailand was only a brief reprieve from the chaos that was the nebulous Thai-Burmese border in late 1980s and 1990s. Ten of thousands of ethnic minorities were fleeing the regime in Rangoon while, simultaneously, thousands of ethnic Burmese dissidents were fleeing the brutal crackdown following the 8888 Uprising. Like many, the Htoos settled in makeshift villages with other Karen just inside the Thai border. There they reunited with Brown's sister Htoo Htoo and her family, who had fled months prior.

According to Sandy Barron and others, from 1984 until 1998, the settlements along the border resembled villages and were relatively self-sufficient. International Non-governmental Organizations (INGOs) were severely restricted by the Royal Thai Government (RTG) from these early camps. During this period, these "displaced persons" maintained their ethnic identity and lived much as they did in Burma but officially inside Thai borders.[18] By this time, the Thai government had been absorbing refugee from Laos and Cambodia. It seems they were less willing to turn a blind eye to the flows coming from Burma and allowed these resettlements to grow.

The Htoos spent the first months in Thailand seeking safety in these encampments. Like others, they were in constant fear of cross-border attacks. Brown and his sister Htoo Htoo recounted the insecurity and terror of those times. The recently formed DKBA and the Tatmadaw ran sorties into Thailand to fight KNLA soldiers. Karen non-combatants like the Htoos were caught in the crossfire.

The first designated shelter where they found some refuge was Borna settlement. Later they moved to Ta Lah Thaw settlement (neither of these settlement names could be confirmed), both of which came under attack by Burmese and DKBA troops, according to Htoo Htoo. Later, both settlements merged with other settlements and became larger refugee camps. For many like the Htoos, Mae La Camp, the largest of the nine camps along the Thai-Burmese border, was the last haven, which became home for the next twelve years. The Htoos were among the first to be officially registered as refugees in 1999. This official acknowledgment that someone is a "refugee" is an important first step in the path to resettlement.

Seventeen Years in Mae La Camp

In January 2005, the last census before the Htoo family left Mae La for the United States, the nine Thai camps housed approximately 140,000 refugees. Mae La Camp alone accounted for 49,476 at its height in the spring of 2007. Most residents of Mae La Camp are ethnic Karen.[19]

The brothers often related stories of intrigue and fear within the camp. They spoke of how spies for the Burmese Army and DKBA lived within the camps and how Karen and Burmese agents perpetrated occasional assassinations. Others have documented such accounts, most famously the Karen author Zoya Phan. Her autobiography, *Little Daughter*,[20] chronicles her family's journey. Her father, Padoh Mahn Sha Lan Phan, was the Secretary-General of the KNU and was assassinated in Mae Sot, Thailand (the Thai town closest to Mae La Camp) in 2008.

The Htoo brothers also related stories to me that had been told to them by elders about the perils of crossing bridges back into Burma. It seems that parents and grandparents would use the fear of the Tatmadaw to not only dissuade children from any ideas of sneaking out of the camp but as a boogieman of sorts to keep children well behaved. For Brown, the Burmese represented repression, broken promises, and deceit. He often expressed his mistrust of the Burmese, which he passed down to his children. Surprising to me was his lack of trust in Aung San Suu Kyi whom he insisted was in cahoots with the Burmese generals.

The operations of Mae La Camp, in many ways, are a legacy of the Karen colonial experience. Much of what the Karen people had learned about self-governance from the British and missionaries had been applied to their governance of Kawthoolei. Much of that leadership has continued in camps like Mae La. These camps seem to have created their own cultural communities with unique characteristics. I recently talked with a young Karen woman in Sandville who indicated that she could discern which camps someone had lived in based solely on their accent. Many ethnicities have sought refuge in Mae La Camp, but most are ethnic Karen.

Mae La Camp has long sheltered a majority Karen (80 percent according to The Border Consortium [TBC]) population, and many Karen community-based organizations (KCBO) help administer various services. KCBOs include the Karen Women's Organization (KWO), Karen Education and Culture Department (KECD), the Karen Teachers Working

Group (KTG), Karen Refugee Committee (KRC), and the Karen Human Rights Group (KHRG). Sgaw Karen Christian leadership heavily influences these CBOs.[21] The power of groups like the KNU to make policy and govern has created some tensions.

TBC, formerly known as the Thailand Burma Border Consortium (TBBC), is a consortium of nine international NGOs from eight countries that have been responsible for a range of services within the camps. The United States, Canada, Australia, Taiwan, and the European Commission all donate to the TBC.

The Htoos were among the lucky ones to be Karen Christians. They were also fortunate to have been registered early on. Once registered, refugee status provided them not only security but material benefits such as food rations and, later, a chance to resettle. Most of the other Karen who made it into Thailand were not so lucky and lived within Thailand undocumented or unregistered in one of the camps. According to the Geneva Convention:

> A refugee is a person who, owing to well-founded fear of being persecuted for reasons of race, religion, nationality, membership in a particular social group or political opinion, is outside the country of his nationality and is unable, or owing to such fear, is unwilling to avail himself of the protection of that country; or who, not having a nationality and being outside the country of his former habitual residence, is unable or, owing to such fear, is unwilling to return to it.[22]

The Honorable Ashin Moonienda, a Karen Buddhist monk, suggests that many convert to Christianity to gain the benefits afforded those fortunate enough to be registered as refugees. He refers to them as "rice Christians,"[23] converting to Christianity for benefits such as rice rations. Interestingly, Donald Smeaton more than one hundred years earlier also suggested that some Karen convert for material benefits.[24] Over the years, some Karen in the United States have confided in me that the practice of converting for reasons other than religious transformation does occur within the diaspora.

Mae La Camp is divided into zones and resembles a very large village. The Htoos lived in Zone B in a three-room bamboo home set on stilts to avoid flooding in the monsoon season. They had no running water or electricity. Sam Ber Htoo described their home this way:

> It's not same as here [United States], Mr. Dan. We don't have room like living rooms. We have kitchen with a bamboo wall and then a big room we sleep in. Another wall separate where everyone sleep. My brothers sleep in another room. We have no furniture, just sleep on the floor. Everything made with bamboo, even cup for toothbrush. That why many Karen sleep in the same room in the US.[25]

I have found that some Karen families in the United States often continue to sleep in the same room and reimagine how a home is utilized. For example, a "living room" may become a large bedroom that sleeps a whole family. And the Karen in Sandville still cook many meals in outdoor kitchens. This may be part of the legacy of housing in the camps and life in Burma. But it is also a pragmatic solution to high heating costs as some families sleep together and heat only one room, and outdoor kitchens save on electricity. I was always fascinated by how families reimagined the idea of home. It also seems that over time, families adapt more American style preferences for independence and children sleep separately once they reach a certain age.

Each zone in Mae La Camp supports a school, a church, some private shops, and some administrative buildings, according to the Htoos. Today, Mae La has Internet services and there are many videos available on YouTube that provide a sense of conditions. Today, the UNHCR is responsible for registration and works alongside TBC in supervising and coordinating operations within the camp.

In addition to receiving food rations of rice, salt, and fish paste, the Htoos were provided health care and clothing, and a limited amount of cooking fuel. The Htoos periodically raised a few pigs and chickens beneath their home for consumption or sale and had a small parcel of land they farmed beside their house.

Officially, education in Mae La was provided until grade 10, but no vocational training was offered. As of 2021, more educational opportunities exist. The Htoo brothers and other Karen interviewed in my various research projects often spoke about education in the camps as something requiring payment, but no official TBC records state as much. Despite the hardships of living in such conditions, the primary complaint of Brown and other Karen adults was the lack of employment, freedom of movement, and uncertainty.

Due to tense relations between the Thai government and refugees, employment opportunities were extremely limited. A refugee could face deportation if found working illegally in Thailand, according to Brown Htoo. Despite the risk, Brown and other Mae La residents often worked on local Thai fields harvesting crops and often crossed into Burma to harvest bamboo, hunt, or make charcoal for sale and personal use. Despite the safety and basic provisions provided, life in the camps offered few legal employment or higher education opportunities. However, each of the Htoo children received some formal education while at Mae La.

Despite the obvious hardships associated with being born and raised within a refugee camp, the Htoo brothers have only spoken disparagingly about the lack of food, the strict teachers, the smell of the toilets, and the difficulty lugging water from one of the public taps. Even so, they often spoke fondly of their memories of life in Mae La Camp, recounting warm memories of their friendships, play, and their "illegal" forays beyond the camp's borders. The only picture of the family in the camps offers a glimpse of four skinny but smiling brothers (see figure 2.2).

The ultimate goal is resettlement for many refugees, but I have no sense that the Htoos had ever considered resettlement a possibility until just a few weeks before applying. Once resettlement became an option, a frenzy began within the camps. Again, Sam Ber Htoo described the scene:

> When people know they can come to America everything change in Mae La. All people want to come to US. Many people even want to kill to try and come. Some family they buy the other family names. Really! Many people in the camp with money they buy the name so they can come here [US]. It crazy what people do. Some family not even Karen people but they pretend to be another family. Some people Burmese people![26]

Resettlement to the United States

More than 3 million refugees have been resettled in the United States since 1985.[27] The United States first formalized refugee resettlement via the passage of the Refugee Act in 1980. Since that time, the United States has become the world leader in providing refuge to individuals and families from at least seventy countries of origin.[28] According to Kelly Jeffreys and Daniel Martin's report for the Office of Immigration Statistics (OIS), in 2007, the year the Htoos arrived in the United States, the government resettled 48,217 refugees. Burmese refugees accounted for 13,896 or approximately 30 percent of all refugees resettled that year.[29]

The Bush administration's decision in 2006 to allow Karen resettlement to the United States was ostensibly made because of the administration's change of heart toward the KNU and the KNLA. Before 2006, the US government viewed the KNU as a terrorist organization. It thus precluded Karen resettlement to the United States prior to 2006.[30]

Before 2006, most Karen were barred from resettlement because of their "material" support for the KNLA. Then Secretary of State Condoleezza Rice waived the Patriot Act terrorist provisions that were precluding Karen resettlement.[31] Though the Htoos were proponents of the mission of the KNU and the KNLA, none had served in either group. The US government claimed that this resettlement program was motivated by the human rights crises along the Thai-Burmese border. However, the reality may be largely due to the long historical connections between American missionaries and the Karen people. Jeremy Zremski, writing for *The Buffalo News*,

Figure 2.2. Four of the Htoo brothers, Mae La Refugee Camp. © Daniel Gilhooly

attributes the United States' change of heart regarding Burmese refugees to then First Lady Laura Bush's "obsession" with Burmese refugees.[32] His article "Laura Bush: A Hero to the Refugees from Burma" suggests that the First Lady was instrumental in changing governmental policy on refugees from Burma.

Like other refugees, the resettlement process was confusing and uncertain for the Htoos. They were among the first to apply for resettlement and were somewhat fast-tracked, as they had already been registered with the UNHCR. In 2006, the Htoos applied for resettlement with many of Brown Htoo's relatives, namely his daughter and her family, along with his sister Htoo Htoo, her four adult sons, and her young daughter. However, others in their extended family stayed in Mae La or resettled in Australia, Canada, New Zealand, and Norway. Esther's siblings have been resettled in South Carolina, Washington State, Wisconsin, as well as in Australia.

The Htoos were referred to the International Rescue Committee (IRC), which processes applications for the US government. They were then scheduled for an interview with IRC. After a background check, the family's information was handed over to the US Department of Homeland Security (DHS), which conducted a final interview. With no criminal record, the Htoos were accepted for resettlement by DHS in early 2017.

Once they were approved for resettlement, the family completed medical checks and prepared for their journey to Phoenix, Arizona, where they were assigned. It is unclear from the family's explanation but their paperwork seems to indicate a delay in their resettlement date due to the health concerns of Brown Htoo. The family spoke of his hospitalization in Phoenix, but I have never been able to verify the cause of his hospitalization.

Days prior to leaving Thailand, the family received the aforementioned cultural orientation that included information about Western-style amenities and other issues related to American weather, work, and housing. According to Sam Ber Htoo, the short information session jokingly amounted to "how to use a toilet." They were also provided some "survival" English classes. The IOM handled all their travel arrangements for the US government and was responsible for the safe transfer of the Htoos to their final destination.

The family packed their belongings into four bags, including: donated clothing, two family Bibles, a machete, a hammer, a Karen dictionary, some music CDs, some medicine, and a single photo from life in the camps. The day before their departure to the United States, the Htoos and three other families were driven from Mae La to Bangkok for their flight. The brothers often described, with great excitement, their hotel stay the night before departure. I can only imagine the thrill they experienced having come directly from the camps. Even a modest Bangkok hotel would have seemed a luxurious world far from Mae La. On 2 September 2007, the family left Thailand from Bangkok's Don Mueang Airport bound for Phoenix via stopovers in Hong Kong and Los Angeles.

Phoenix, Arizona

Upon arrival at Phoenix Sky Harbor International Airport, the Htoos were greeted by a volunteer from Lutheran Social Ministries and settled into a fully furnished apartment with a full pantry and basic amenities. Their new home was in a modest section of Phoenix, just off Interstate 17. According to RealtyTrac, an online resource for real estate data,[33] the neighborhood has a moderately high crime rate, and the schools are listed as "poor." The brothers often spoke of how scared they were to leave the house, which made me wonder about the neighborhood's safety. They each described their apartment complex as a mix of refugees from Burma, Iraq, and Somalia. While they never experienced any crime, they each expressed a reluctance to go outside, and Sam Ber Htoo often chided his brothers for their unwillingness to speak English that first year.

From the start, refugees brought to the United States begin their American experience in debt. According to the US Committee for Refugees and Immigrants (USCRI), families like the Htoos are required to repay the US government for their airfare within five years of arriving.[34] In the case of the Htoos, they owed nearly $7,000. The Htoos, like other Karen I have interviewed and spoken with, paid their debt within the first two years by borrowing from friends and saving. The family expressed concern that they might be deported if they failed to pay. In reality, failure to repay the government can impair credit history, but not lead to deportation. Making refugee families repay airfare is still a head-scratcher for me. The wealthiest country on the planet cannot foot the bill for airfare for the most vulnerable people at one of their most vulnerable moments?

Brown and Esther took English classes for the first few months but had to quit their studies due to the need to find employment. As Noor Daewood suggests in his article in the *Berkeley Public Policy Journal*, the US government's demand for self-sufficiency comes at a high cost, as refugees do not have the requisite time to learn the language and begin to adapt.[35]

In Phoenix, the brothers started school in January 2008, three months after arriving. Brown bussed tables part-time at a Chinese restaurant and stocked shelves at a Dollar Store. Esther was a housekeeper at a Phoenix hotel. As hard as I try, I just cannot imagine Brown Htoo in an apron bussing tables. It just does not compute. The Brown Htoo I have known is a man of the land: a hunter, a trapper, a cook, a gardener, and a man who loved to talk. This rush to self-sufficiency seems unrealistic. Again, Noor Daewood unpacks some of the other ramifications of US policy to get refugees working as soon as possible. He writes:

> By requiring that newly arrived refugees pursue immediate employment, the government compromises refugees' ability to recover from physical and emotional trauma and to adapt to their new surroundings. Further, this policy deprives refugees of opportunities to acquire knowledge, skills, and credentials necessary to ensure long-term economic prosperity. Refugees are consequently channeled into the same circumstances that plague the nation's poor, thus perpetuating experiences of hardship for themselves, their communities, and broader US society.[36]

The Htoos, as we shall see, are very much products of the system.

Refugees are a unique classification from other immigrants and are afforded certain benefits. According to the US Department of State: "Refugees receive employment authorization upon arrival and are encouraged to become employed as soon as possible."[37] Refugees become permanent residents upon arrival and can become citizens after five years. It took the entire Htoo family fourteen years to become naturalized citizens. This could have been expedited if Brown or Esther had become citizens earlier. Any child under the age of eighteen is naturalized when their parents naturalize. However, like many older refugee resettlers, Brown and Esther worried whether or not they could pass the naturalization test, so they kept delaying until they finally were naturalized in 2020.

The Htoos expressed a liking for Phoenix but were weary of city life. Despite a growing Karen community in Phoenix, Brown and Esther longed for the familiarity of rural life. There was also talk between Brown and the president of the Karen Baptist Churches in the United States (KBCUSA) of establishing an ethnoreligious community in rural Georgia.

Brown Htoo left Phoenix on 2 September 2008 (one year to the day after his arrival in the United States) for Georgia with his nephew, Hsa Kpor, and his son Moe Tha Wah to start work and get established. After the two-day drive, they arrived in Sandville, Georgia. Through his nephew Eh Kaw, Brown Htoo first found seasonal employment on a farm where he cut wood and harvested crops. Four months later, during the children's summer break, Esther and the boys arrived in Sandville with Brown's sister Htoo Htoo, her husband Kyaw Mint, and their nine-year-old daughter Eh Ku Htoo.

Notes

Epigraph: According to *Karen Proverbs*, this Karen proverb means "Staying together in peace brings happiness." Drum Publications, *Karen Proverbs*, 25.

 1. Brown, *Our Words Are Very Little*, 46.
 2. Brown, *Our Words Are Very Little*, 48.
 3. Thawnghmung, *The "Other" Karen*, 36.
 4. See Gilhooly and Htoo, 2022.
 5. Zan, *Life's Journey in Faith*.
 6. Po, *Burma and Karens*, xxix.
 7. Thawnghmung, *The "Other" Karen*.
 8. These four principles were written on a t-shirt the brothers' gifted me.
 9. Lee, *Adaptation and Identities*, 79.
10. Falla, *True Love and Bartholomew*, xix.
11. Smith, *Fifty Years*,17.
12. She was named after the biblical Esther. Esther added Htoo as a surname after coming to the United States.
13. Smith, *State of Strife*.
14. Barron et al., *Refugees from Burma*, 7.
15. Kunz, "Refugee in Flight," 126.

16. Malseed, "Networks of Noncompliance."
17. Heppner, "Sold to Be Soldiers," 102–3.
18. Bowles, "From Village to Camp."
19. Thawnghmung, *The "Other" Karen*.
20. Published in the United States under the title, *Undaunted: My Struggle for Freedom and Survival in Burma.*
21. South, "Karen Nationalist Communities," 11.
22. McBrien, "Educational Needs and Barriers," 333.
23. Moonieinda, *Karen People*, 30.
24. Smeaton, *Loyal Karens*, 190.
25. Interview, Sam Ber, November 12, 2011.
26   Interview, Sam Ber, February 16, 2011.
27. Nezer, *Resettlement at Risk*, 4.
28. Daewood, "Persecution to Poverty."
29. Jefferys and Martin, *Refugees and Asylees*, 1–2.
30. Barnett, "A New Era," 6.
31. Barnett, "A New Era," 6.
32. Zremski, "Laura Bush."
33. RealtyTrac. Retrieved 29 June 2022 from https://www.realtytrac.com/.
34. "Travel Loan Services."
35. Daewood, "Persecution to Poverty."
36. Daewood, "Persecution to Poverty."
37. "U.S. Refugee Admissions Program: Reception and Placement."

Chapter 3

Home

Sandville, Georgia, USA

> A large deer in its territory, a small deer at its saltlick.
>
> —Karen proverb

More than 95 percent of all refugees arriving in the United States are resettled in urban areas.[1] However, most refugees arriving are from rural areas in their country of origin. This makes the Htoo's Karen community in Sandville unique.

While push factors influenced the Htoos to leave Phoenix, they were pulled by greater forces. The prospect for better employment, cheap land, the familiarity of rural living, family reunification, safety, and the dream to build a Karen religious community in rural Georgia drew the Htoos and others to Sandville.

The reunited Htoo family initially lived together in Sandville, Georgia, a ninety-minute drive from Atlanta. Greater Atlanta has become a center for many Karen. Clarkston, Georgia, has become synonymous with refugees and is known colloquially as the American South's Ellis Island. Sandville is a rural community of just under a thousand people located among the rolling hills of eastern Georgia twenty minutes from the South Carolina-Georgia state line. The community was once a thriving agricultural area but today is home to a dilapidated volunteer fire department, a Baptist church, and a handful of granite quarries. The nearest town with a grocery store is eleven miles away, as are the county's elementary, middle, and high schools.

Karen Origins in Sandville

Karen families originally migrated to Sandville due to its proximity to Jubilee Partners, a non-denominational intentional Christian service community working with resettled refugees. The first Karen to live in the area, Eh Kaw (Brown's nephew), was resettled by Jubilee Partners in 2006. After a brief move to Atlanta, he returned to the area to work for Jubilee as a translator in 2007. His relocation to the region sparked the growth of the Sgaw Karen community that continues to grow today. Before 2014, all of the Karen of Sandville were either related to the Htoo family or were friends from the camps or Phoenix.

Sandville, Georgia

The Sandville Karen community is singular for two reasons. First, as noted above, unlike most resettled refugee communities who are resettled in urban areas, Sandville represents one of the few rural Karen communities in the United States. Second, two institutions have supported the community—the Karen Baptist Churches of the United States of America (KBCUSA) and the aforementioned Jubilee Partners. In 2012, the president of KBCUSA moved to Sandville with his family from Phoenix. His presence has connected Sandville to regional, national, and international Karen church organizations, making Sandville a hub despite its rural isolation.

The network of church groups under the auspices of the KBCUSA offers members spiritual support and financial support in times of crisis. After Hurricane Harvey hit Houston, KCBUSA assisted affected Karen families. For Sandville, the KBCUSA has been a place of worship and a community gathering social space. The community hopes to build a missionary school on the more than twenty acre grounds one day. The Htoos often hosted missionaries visiting the area to preach and inform about the latest news from Burma, the camps, and other KBCUSA communities in the United States.

The support provided by Jubilee Partners, a non-denominational Christian service community that resettles small numbers of refugees, has also been a critical component in the development of the Sandville Karen community and the neighboring Karen community of Pineville (pseudonym). Jubilee has helped the Karen and other resettlers find employment, study English, and connect to area churches. Jubilee is located on 200 acres of land and has become a space for religious and cultural events for Karen and other ethnic groups from Burma and Africa.

In 2009, after a season of harvesting crops in the area, the nascent Karen community began to look for more permanent employment. Those early Karen resettlers, like Brown and Moe Tha Wah, traded in their work under the hot Georgia sun for more secure employment in one of the nearby poultry processing facilities, a euphemism for a chicken slaughterhouse. However, Brown Htoo was the only adult Karen applicant unable to secure employment due to a past injury that impacted his ability to grip certain machinery. As a result, Esther and their eldest son Moe Tha Wah became the breadwinners in the Htoo family. They worked eight- to ten-hour shifts six days a week for $9.00 an hour deboning chicken from March 2009 until their move to Iowa in May 2012.

The Htoo Home

Most of my teaching and socializing with the Htoo family was at their home in Sandville. The Htoo's rented house resembled a southern-style shotgun house with a front porch with a narrow body that extended away from the road. This home originally housed Brown and twelve other Karen. The home is where I taught the Htoo brothers from May 2010 until May 2012.

The seven-room house consisted of a bathroom, a kitchen, and a living room, while the other four rooms had been converted into makeshift bedrooms. The home had no immediate neighbors but was located across the street from Sandville Baptist Church. When I met the Htoos in May 2010, Brown Htoo, Esther Htoo, Moe Tha Wah, Sam Ber Htoo, Hser Gay Htoo, Hse Ku Htoo, and Ler Moo occupied the home. The three oldest boys had their own bedrooms in the back of the house while Hser Ku Htoo slept in the family TV room, and Ler Moo slept in his parent's room. The rent was $450.00 per month until their final few months there when it was reduced to $425.00 in the spring of 2012.

The house was sparsely furnished with very few decorations other than a calendar from an Asian grocery, a few printed pictures of the brothers, and a laminated map of the United States taped to the living room wall. The living room housed an old wooden desk holding a desktop computer and a heavily used sofa that was rarely sat upon, as most everyone opted to sit or lie on the wooden floors. The house had neither air-conditioning nor a working furnace. In the summer, we escaped the heat and studied in the relative cool of the porch if there was a breeze. We studied bundled in layers of jackets and winter hats in the winter.

The house had imperfections that caused the family minor inconveniences. The family spent over a month without running water due to a burst pipe, but they adapted and never seemed all that inconvenienced.

Later, during the preparations for the eldest brother Moe Tha Wah's wedding, the septic tank overflowed, and they had no working toilet for over a month. Yet, an American "friend" from church invariably addressed these and other issues. The brothers were most concerned with the availability of Wi-Fi that they surreptitiously accessed from the pastor's house adjacent to the church across the street.

The kitchen had a gas stove and a round wooden dining room table with five chairs for a family of six. These chairs were carried to the living room or front porch for our study sessions. There was always a pot of rice in the rice cooker and side dishes prepared by Esther, Brown, or Hser Ku Htoo available whenever anyone was hungry. A stone mortar, pestle, and various spices, namely turmeric and red pepper, sat on the counter. The smell of turmeric and cooked rice always hung in the air.

A homemade eighteen-inch machete usually sat atop the kitchen counter and was the primary tool for cutting everything from vegetables to large sides of goat and pig. A sharpening stone was also readily available on the countertop. The kitchen also housed an aging refrigerator, a microwave (used as a storage box), and a wall-mounted telephone. The kitchen was always kept clean; everyone was responsible for cleaning their dishes after every meal. The kitchen floor always contained at least a few fifty-pound sacks of long grain rice from Sam's Club stacked in the corner.

In the early days of teaching the Htoos brothers, I read Harry Marshall's 1922 ethnography on the Karen. It was my first foray into an academic text on the Karen, and I marveled at the level of detail and was struck by the similarities between what I was observing and Marshall's account. His description of Karen eating habits so precisely captures a scene I saw played out so many times I must include it here.

> The serving of food among the Karen is a simple matter. The rice is emptied into a tray, the meats or vegetables are put in little bowls, and all are set on a mat on the floor. The members of the household squat around the family board and eat with the hand. They pour gravy from the meat, fish, or other side dishes on the rice, work it with the fingers, and convey the food in compact lumps to their mouth. . . . There is not much sociability about a Karen meal. Each person attends to his eating until he is finished, when he rises, rinses off his hands, quenches his thirst with a drink of water, and withdraws to sit down, or leaves the house without formality.[2]

For most meals, the Htoo family sat at a table rather than the floor, but all else matches completely with the scenes I found in other nineteenth-century accounts. Though the writing is dated, patronizing, judgmental, and sexist, for someone experiencing nearly the exact same scene a hundred years later and 8,000 miles away from Burma, I felt as if I was part of something remarkable and timeless.

The Yard

The front porch, where we often studied, faced a paved country road that turned to dirt a few hundred meters down. The porch was always replete with an assortment of shoes. Some shoes were organized on a makeshift shoe rack while others lay scattered, the only external sign of the inhabitants within. Their acre of property housed a garden, which, when in season, primarily consisted of red pepper and a few tobacco plants. A row of sunflowers was used to block the view of the tobacco plants from the road. When I commented one day about the beauty of the sunflowers, the boys smiled sheepishly and said they were planted to "hide" the tobacco from the church. Brown rolled his cigarettes but seemed to think it unseemly to the American Baptist congregants across the road.

Each of the Karen homes in Sandville maintains gardens of various sizes replete with various Southeast Asian vegetables. While all homes grew red peppers like the Htoos, other Karen families diversified and grew enormous fuzzy squash dangling from bamboo trellises, neat rows of long beans hanging from bamboo lattices, lush taro plants with their elephantine leaves, and other vegetables and herbs.

Beside the Htoo house, two freestanding portable basketball hoops, left by a former tenant, stood in a large dirt parking area that accommodated the cars of all the Karen visitors from as far away as Burma. A large fenced-in backyard was home to roughly twenty to thirty free-range chickens, three roosters, and two geese. Before weddings or festivals, two or three goats could be found tethered to the fence in their backyard awaiting slaughter.

The fenced backyard consisted primarily of hardened dirt stained with blood from slaughtering animals and chicken feathers with a few small patches of grass that spoke of greener days. The yard was untidy and not meant for recreation or entertainment and was usually littered with flotsam and jetsam of rural Georgia. Two homemade tables used for butchering animals were constructed from old wooden doors. The chickens were periodically slaughtered and eaten but were primarily kept as sources of fresh eggs. Others were sold to newly arrived Karen families. According to Sam Ber Htoo, a pair of geese were kept because Esther "liked to look at them" as they reminded her of her native home in Burma.

Sandville Baptist Church

The Htoos were very active in their local church. The first church they and the other Karen in Sandville attended was Sandville Baptist, located across from the Htoo home. Until 2013, the Karen community congregated alongside their white neighbors at Sandville Baptist. The Karen mostly sat in the back as a group, but their chorus sang regularly at the ten o'clock service. Brown and other elders had hoped they could finish building a Karen church complex by 2013 to celebrate Judson's arrival in Burma, but they had to wait. In 2013, the Karen community rented a small vacant church three miles from the Htoo house. Starting in 2012, Karen families pooled their money and bought connected parcels of land for mobile homes and their future church complex.

The proximity of the Htoo home to Sandville Baptist Church provided me access to the entire Karen community, who often visited before or after church services and on special occasions. All the Karen of Sandville were members of Sandville Baptist Church, a primarily white congregation of nearly a hundred congregants. Sandville Baptist's pastor, Pastor Rus (pseudonym), and a few other families acted as ad hoc caseworkers.

Pastor Rus was instrumental in encouraging community support for their new Karen neighbors and was a key catalyst in the successful resettlement of Karen in the area. Beyond his religious duties, he has helped each family buy land, procure housing, access Supplemental Nutrition Assistance Program (SNAP), access medical assistance, acquire large machinery for clearing land, and negotiate loans.

I attended a few services and two Karen weddings over the years at Sandville Baptist. One memorable service I attended was for Mother's Day in 2011. Pastor Rus gave me my first glimpse into the politics of the all-white congregation. Pastor Rus asked his congregants for examples of righteous mothers who stood as models of faith and religiosity. A few congregants shouted names unfamiliar to me, and Pastor Rus concurred. With little transition, he began to preach against other less worthy women, and somehow, Oprah was thrown into the mix!

Brown Htoo's Life in Sandville

Brown Htoo is a master hunter, trapper, and fisherman. Some game was being pursued, prepared, or preserved more often than not. Brown was a frequent squirrel hunter in all weather, and the family often fished at a local muddy creek for crappie and catfish with Huck Finn-like bamboo poles and a few meters of line. When fishing in local lakes, the preferred method was a throw-net. No fish was too small to eat or make a fish paste with, and there were often jars of fermenting fish on the kitchen counter or left to ferment in the backyard.

Brown was often in the backyard with his .22 rifle looking for quarry, namely anything that flew and squirrel. Georgia squirrel was a favorite dish among some in the family and gained a reputation across the Karen diaspora. Once, as I sat talking with the brothers, a Karen preacher from Burma pulled up with, I later found out, her "bodyguard," and the first thing they said was, "Is there any squirrel?" at which everyone laughed. Other experiences with squirrels were equally funny, at least for some.

The local post office was traumatized when Brown tried to send relatives in Wisconsin thirty burnt squirrels haphazardly thrown in a box. He was told, very politely, by a bewildered postal worker that the US Postal Service did not allow shipping squirrel by mail. Interestingly, Max and Bertha Ferrars noted this appreciation of squirrels in their 1900 accounts of the Karen people![3] On other days, Brown would have an assortment of songbirds laid out on an old metal yield sign he used to clean smaller game.

The burning of game, like squirrels, and sun-drying meat were the primary means of preserving meat. Often, strips of meat were left to dry on blue tarps, flattened cardboard boxes, lined along the tops of fences, or laid out on the roof to dry under the Georgia sun. The burning of squirrels was so ubiquitous that it became the running-joke name of my cane ball team—The Burning Squirrels!

Whether it was goat being prepared for a wedding feast or the annual Sweet December celebration, Brown always threw the carcass atop a fire in the backyard with the nonchalance of a pit-master. Once the hair was singed, it was removed, disemboweled, hacked up, and thrown in a boiling pot atop a fire. I imagine such scenes playing out in villages throughout Burma, the camps, and those throughout the Karen diaspora lucky enough to have space and privacy for the operation.

The Htoos were not averse to picking up luckless animals from the side of the road, and it became an informal competition within the community to see who would be first to retrieve the latest victim. The brothers would have me pull over if we spotted any fresh roadkill before one of their relatives got to it first. A group of Karen men did quick work butchering any size animal. Over time, the community realized the illegality of hunting without a license and out-of-season and became more discreet about their exploits. While squirrels and deer were the most common quarry, I observed or was told stories, usually from unwitting children, about catching, shooting, or finding; fox, coyote, owl, turtle, opossum, raccoon, and wild pig for dinner. The brothers would joke that the Karen would eat anything with four legs, except a table! The only exception I noted was an unwillingness to eat crow or buzzards.

Brown Htoo was an expert trapper and fashioned snares out of thin bamboo strips as he had during his missionary days in Burma and later outside the refugee camps. One day he demonstrated the efficacy of three traps. He fashioned three separate traps and demonstrated how they worked on felling a variety of prey. Others in the community designed ingenious traps made from pine logs fashioned in such a way as to crush unwitting prey tempted into the garden.

Brown Htoo is solid muscle despite his diminutive frame, works tirelessly in his garden, and goes hunting regularly. He was and is a respected elder in the community and continues to be active in the Karen church. Despite only a few years of formal education, he is multilingual. He can read, speak, and write Burmese and Pwo Karen in addition to his native Sgaw Karen. His sons claim he can read in English, but I never witnessed him reading any English text. I have only heard him utter *hello* and *thank you* in English, and on my most recent phone call, I heard *I love you* a few times.

Brown Htoo is renowned in the family and the Karen community as a great storyteller. Many afternoons were spent with him recounting stories to me with Sam Ber Htoo interpreting. He talked about life in Burma, his exploits hunting in the jungle, and stories of spirits, spells, and the supernatural.

Myth, Legends, and the Supernatural

His stories of the supernatural were held onto with as much fervor and resolve as his certainty of Christ's resurrection. My use of the word *supernatural* is strictly mine. I imagine Brown, like Sam Ber Htoo, would consider these to be obvious truths about the natural world. While some of these stories were lost in translation, I received others with such incredulity or astonishment as to always lead to a heated exchange with Sam Ber Htoo on the veracity of his and his dad's claims.

During the first months working with the Htoos, these stories were a fascination of mine. These were the days when everything was new to me, and I was an eager questioner and listener. Later, I would question these stories to get the brothers thinking about the veracity of such beliefs. These stories would come up as a natural part of a conversation most of the time and became a major topic of conversation between Sam Ber Htoo and me. The other brothers listened intently but rarely offered an opinion. They seemed caught between two worlds. My reasoning seemed to make sense to them, but they were also intrigued and interested by their father's stories.

After reviewing my field notes and audio files on these interactions, I would often return to Brown with more questions. I would often ask Brown, through Sam Ber, to clarify or verify my notes or understanding from an earlier explanation. Each of these exchanges inevitably ended with Sam Ber Htoo, recognizing my skepticism, emphatically exclaiming, "No, no, Mr. Dan! It true! Ask any Karen people! It true!" I did ask other Karen, and some had heard similar tales, while others were just as puzzled as me. I call the first of these stories the *matchbox baby* for lack of a better descriptor.

The Matchbox Baby, Baby Hats, and Shrinking

The matchbox baby story was one I checked and rechecked with the Htoos. According to Sam Ber Htoo, a woman in the camps bore a matchbox-sized, fully developed (the child was described as fully formed but in miniature) lifeless baby. It always conjured up a shrunken head in my mind when he described such a baby. For Brown, possessing such a baby is seen as propitious, a charm of sorts. Sam Ber Htoo related how a young Karen woman from the camps carried such a baby in a matchbox while traveling illegally in Thailand. He believed that the baby helped her evade Thai military checkpoints and delivered her to her destination safely. Such a matchbox baby was also said to have provided owners winning numbers for the lottery. After some research, I assume he was referring to a stillbirth of some kind.

Brown Htoo also related the propitiousness of a baby born with a hat. "A hat!" I exclaimed. "I have never heard of a baby born with a hat," I retorted doubtfully. But an animated Sam Ber Htoo held fast in his belief. After speaking with my mother, a former nurse and a mother of eleven children herself, I later realized that what he was most likely describing was a birth caul that may resemble a hat and is often associated with superstitions across many cultures.[4]

Another miniature story arose one day after some paperwork I had brought to their home slipped out of my bag and fell through a crack in their porch. Sam Ber Htoo suggested we find a cat and extract its liver, which, he related, would help us shrink down to be able to slide through the crack and retrieve the papers. Sam Ber Htoo half-smiled when he told me this, and I was unsure whether or not it was something he believed or not despite his insistence that it was true.

Another miniature story involves a tiny white elephant the size of a marble. Again, according to Brown via Sam Ber Htoo, such miniature white elephants are found on the banks of rivers, and the possessor is said to be able to tame a regular-sized elephant. This is interesting because the Karen were renowned mahouts (elephant handlers) in the region.

Tattoos

While neither Brown nor his sons had permanent tattoos (all the brothers had self-drawn pen tattoos at various times), Karen tattoos are common in the United States.[5] It seems that for Brown's generation, tattoos were believed to have supernatural powers. Brown's sister Htoo Htoo's brother-in-law, James, was the renowned Karen rebel fighter I referenced earlier. He was said to have defied death many times because of his stomach tattoo. I was told all sorts of heroic tales by Brown and James's daughter about his exploits killing Burmese troops. It seems that his tattoo made him impervious to Burmese bullets for years, until one day it did not—and he was brutally killed. One story related to me explained that he died from a shot to the leg, an area of his body unprotected by the tattoo. Another report claimed that the charm finally failed him because he had "sinned," or some other indiscretion.

Curses

The sole story told to me of the supernatural occurring to someone in the United States was the story of Moo Moo (pseudonym), the brothers' maternal cousin. Moo Moo was a teenager living with her parents and two teenage brothers in Columbia, South Carolina. Her adjustment was difficult, and Hser Gay Htoo described her as shy and lonely. Her luck changed when, one day, a male classmate befriended her. They soon became best friends. It seems that this friend asked her to be his girlfriend, and, for whatever reason, she declined. She most likely denied him because, as it was described to me, "Karen don't date." Whatever the reason, it appears that the young man took it badly, and the two friends stopped talking.

Soon after, Moo Moo started to act strangely, what Hser Gay called "crazy." According to an animated Sam Ber Htoo, who had recently heard the story from her adolescent brothers, she began to stare into space, stopped helping her mother with chores, stopped eating, and was always yelling at her brothers. When I suggested that such a description might be made of all sisters at some point, they responded with incredulity at my ignorance. "No, no, Mr. Dan!" exhorted an exasperated Sam Bser Htoo. "He do a . . . [Sam Ber Htoo paused not knowing the word and then searched his Karen dictionary] *curse*! He curse her because she don't like him like that. She crazy now! He mad she not like him and [refers back to the dictionary] curse her and now she crazy."

Other tales and legends have been related to me, but they are for another book. For now, I will return to my account of Brown in Sandville.

In addition to speaking with me, Brown was often found on the telephone in heated conversations about the situation in Burma, the camps, and the changes the community was facing in the United States. Unlike many of his generation, he never served in any insurgency groups fighting against the government, but he was an avid consumer of news from home. It was clear he supported the Karen cause but, like many, was losing hope that the Karen cause would prevail any time soon.

Most days, when not outside hunting or tending the garden, he was often sprawled out on the floor or, in winter, wrapped up in blankets in

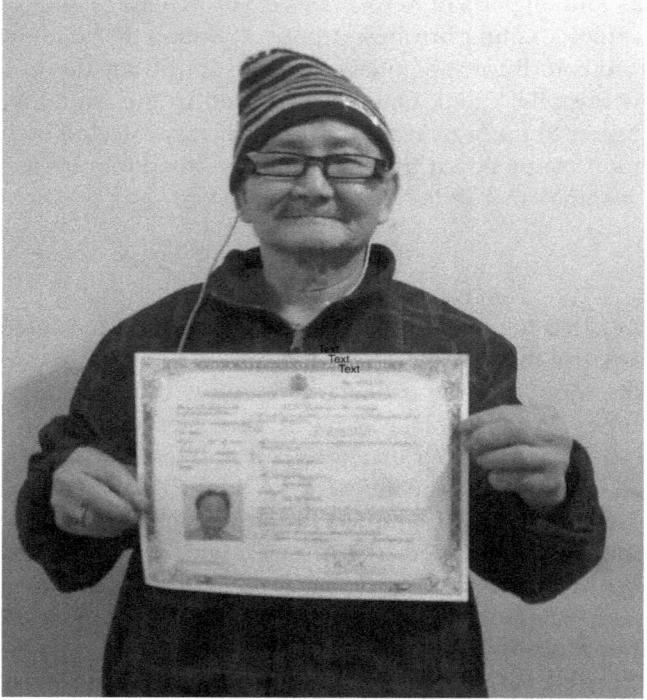

Figure 3.1. Brown Htoo and his naturalization certificate (2021). © Daniel Gilhooly

bed listening to the BBC Burma broadcast via the Internet. We often spoke via one of his sons about his feelings about the civil war and his pessimism about the future. He was unwavering in his mistrust of the Burmese and often expressed his misgivings about Aung Saan Su Kyi, whom he viewed as in cahoots with the Burmese government. The few times I related the high regard for Aung Saan Su Kyi in the West (at least before 2011), I was met with an awkward silence.

A Man of Faith

Most notably, Brown Htoo is a man of religion, a devout Christian with a knack for preaching. He was recorded preaching over two hours unabated without a script and very few pauses at a Karen-style birthday party (the word "party" is used very loosely) where prayers and preaching abound! Periodically, he would address me directly about my faith with a firmness that caught me off guard. "My dad want to know why you not accept Jesus and talk more about Jesus." Sam Ber Htoo would interpret. I never knew what to say. Brown was steadfast about his beliefs and often implored me to accept Jesus Christ as my savior despite knowing I was baptized and raised Catholic. As committed as Brown was to his faith, I was more ambivalent in mine, and our relationship was always cordial, but at times, I sensed he was displeased with my lack of faith.

My relationship with Brown began rather auspiciously with Brown associating me with the "lost white brother" (described in chapter 1) whom God sent to help free the Karen people. He expressed as much in one of our earliest meetings. He later suggested that I would be a leader within the Karen community once they had defeated the Burmese and the Karen people had reclaimed their rightful places as kings of Southeast Asia.

Today, when I return to Georgia, he often embraces me and is welcoming, while at other visits, he seems withdrawn and barely acknowledges me. On my last visit in May 2021, he was full of energy and enthusiastically sat me down to my favorite meal of turmeric pork chunks, rice, and cucumber salad. It felt like coming home. He also proudly displayed his naturalization certificate and asked me to photograph him.

Esther Htoo

During the two years I visited the Htoo home, Esther worked at the poultry plant alongside her son, Moe Tha Wah, and nearly a hundred other Karen from Sandville, Pineville, and Athens, Georgia, and Karen from as far away as Atlanta. The work is hard, and you are confined to an assembly line in cold conditions that take a toll on the employees. Over those years, I saw her health seem to decline. While Esther looked tired, she enjoyed Sundays with her family and never seemed defeated. Because of her busy schedule, I had few chances to interview her or interact with her as I did with Brown. Seeing their mom work such long hours affected the brothers, and I think it was one of the primary motivators that got them out of bed each morning to catch the school bus at 6:00 a.m. and inspired them to study with me each week.

Chjaw Wah (Older White Brother): Friendship as Rapport

In chapter 15, "Deep Play: Notes on the Balinese Cockfight," of Clifford Geertz's seminal anthropological series of select essays, *The Interpretation of Cultures* (1973), the acclaimed anthropologist describes how a single event helped him and his wife gain rapport among the Balinese villagers they were intending to study. Their escape from a police raid on an illegal cockfight alongside other villagers led to what Geertz describes as: "a sudden and unusually complete acceptance into a society extremely difficult for outsiders to penetrate. It gave me the kind of immediate, inside-view grasp of an aspect of 'peasant mentality' that anthropologists not fortunate enough to flee headlong with their subjects from armed authorities normally do not get."[6]

I am among those outsiders not lucky enough to have had such an immediate and complete acceptance. I cannot trace my rapport with the Htoo family to a single event. Moreover, unlike Geertz and Hilda, I was less fortuitous in gaining rapport so quickly.[7] Gaining rapport took time and, as the development of any friendship, rapport was a process.

Much of the rapport I acquired as teacher-researcher was cemented over countless matches of cane ball.[8] The game is played on a badminton-size court, and rather than a birdie, a hollow cane ball, now commonly made of plastic, about the size of a softball, is kicked back and forth much like any court game where the objective is to gain a point by hitting the ball within your opponent's lines without them able to return. Usually, the game is played three-to-a-side, but we often played matches of two-a-side or, my favorite, one-on-one. It is a game I was familiar with from trips to Thailand and a game I had some skills in from a life playing soccer and many years hacky sacking. Who knew hacky sack would play a role in my academic life?! Cane ball speaks to the importance of finding commonalities with students and research collaborators when building meaningful rapport.

My enthusiasm and ability to play were instrumental in building a relationship apart from my role as a teacher. At first, they were shocked that a teacher, a white guy, could play a game they thought of as uniquely Burmese, Karen, or Thai. It was our first shared interest, and it was something they could assess me on and this, I found, was a step toward developing our friendship. I was also starting to earn some membership as a teammate, opponent, and line judge.

Although I never consciously used cane ball to gain rapport, I realized that these games were helping dismantle the teacher/researcher-student/participant binaries I had hoped to overcome.

Cane Ball and Earning Rapport

As the youngest brother of eleven children and a former athlete, I liked trash-talk. It was an innocent but relentless part of all competition. Ping-Pong, cane ball, or shooting baskets with the Htoo brothers, I acted as I would have with friends and goaded them freely. For many months the brothers stayed stoic at these attempts, and I often wondered if they were comprehending my provocations, and I may have laid it on even thicker in the hope of forcing things a bit. And despite the novelty of this new

Figure 3.2. Author playing cane ball with Htoo brothers (2011). © Daniel Gilhooly

register of English, my tone was clearly provocative. Over time, I could see that my taunts were registering, but the brothers were trapped by centuries of deference to their white brother, and at best, they would only muster a coy but knowing smile.

However, things changed one day during a battle of cane ball that marked a transformation of sorts. Hser Gay Htoo (the middle brother) responded to my taunts with a soft-spoken rebuttal and a knowing smile. He was giving it back to me! On the drive home that day, I could not shake the event, and my field notes were littered with a novice researcher's exultation. I can still see the look on his face in my mind's eye. I had not even heard what he said (Hser Gay was a notorious whisperer those days with very little English language confidence), but his tone, body language, and smile made it clear. I wrote in my field notes that he had said something related to my "getting old," but what has remained is his look. I was delighted, and while I am unsure I met with "complete acceptance" as Geertz and his wife did, it felt as if I had achieved some form of the kind of rapport I envisioned. And cane ball came to represent my unique relationship with the Htoo brothers.

Sam Ber Htoo could never consider talking back, and our relationship was very much one of respect. Sam Ber Htoo always referred to me as a brother, but it was clear I was the older brother, and a distance was between us. Hser Gay Htoo became much more comfortable with English and the role I had assumed, and we found a relationship of laughter, frank discussions, and less formality. He learned to question me, contradict me, and, at times, even challenge me. With Hser Ku Htoo, the next youngest, we built a friendship based on similar views of the world and a shared sense of humor. He was the listener, and his knowing smile conveyed that he knew my taunts were harmless fun. While my relationship with the youngest, Ler Moo, was one of a much older brother and play.

Friendship as Method

While that day provided a memorable anecdote of gaining rapport, building friendships was an ongoing process that involved much more involvement and commitment. I was committed to including the brothers in my life to have them experience me and my life entirely. They met my family, girlfriends, future wife, classmates, and buddies from my past and present. I shared personal and family affairs and how they impacted my views on crime, education, immigration, the criminal justice system, death, politics, race, and religion. These talks and disagreements are the stuff that builds friendship and mutual respect.

Early on in my work with the brothers, I became very much interested in the idea of vulnerability related to teaching and researching. I began considering vulnerability as it relates to relationship building with students and research "participants," who often view both teachers and outside researchers as mythical creatures. Anyone who has run into a teacher for the first time on the street or in the supermarket knows what I am talking about. It is always a bit of a shock to our understanding of the world when that person, whom we came to solely associate with "knowing," "instructing," and "assessing" us in a very particular context, their classroom, is seen attending a movie, shopping at the same grocery as our parents, or out for a walk with their dog. For the brothers, they had the singular chance to not only have one of these rarefied beings in their home, but also have the opportunity to experience him with all his flaws.

It was important and necessary for me to have the brothers experience the totality of me. I believed and still believe this was paramount if I was ever going to build authentic friendships and meaningful collaborations. I remember how touched I was when my teachers shared their personal lives with me and the bonds that created. And emotions like empathy need to be a two-way street, especially with refugee background kids who often only experience sympathy from others. It seems unhealthy and somewhat contrived if those you intend to build relationships with only experience you as a teacher or, even worse, an academic researcher.

At one point, I remember realizing the effect my dilapidated Nissan Altima was having on the brothers. They were amazed that their brother's car was better than their white teacher's car! They joked about it much as my nephews joked about the long list of ailments my trusty Altima endured. If cane ball helped gain rapport, it was my commitment to allowing them to experience enough of me to make a judgment about me that I feel led to our friendship. And our two-week research collaboration helped demystify any status I may have held as the white brother.

It turns out that spending two weeks together is an ideal opportunity for collaborators to experience one another more fully. They experienced my perpetual failed attempts at organization and had front-row seats to my many selves. In those two weeks working together, they each experienced my humor, anger, sharp tongue, sarcasm, and other qualities that you invariably experience traveling with someone but rarely experience with a teacher or "outside" academic.

One episode stands out. On the second day of our drive from Sandville to their uncle's house in Milwaukee to conduct research, I made the fateful decision to stop by and spend a few hours in Chicago. I was excited to show them one of the great cities of the United States, a city I had lived in and was anxious to show off. I was also relieved to be out of the car.

I skipped excitedly up the steps from the parking garage beneath Millennium Park to the sound of a street musician playing the blues on his saxophone. I was giddy to be back in the city and share this experience with them.

My excitement was short-lived. It soon became clear that the brothers were not so excited and very uncomfortable. Ten minutes after our arrival on Michigan Avenue, a chagrined Sam Ber Htoo began asking me, "When we go?" I was angry and indignant. My ethnographer's hat was off, and I snapped, "I drove fourteen hours, and you want to leave Millennium Park on a beautiful day after ten minutes! Holy shit!" I mumbled "Damn it all!" under my breath and begrudgingly walked off. After one look at their downturned heads circling the Bean, I conceded and stomped indignantly back to the car. We drove in silence toward Milwaukee.

I imagine this is the feeling every parent has when they lug their adolescent kids to famed destinations or old haunts only to realize the kid has not lifted their eyes from their iPhone. And indignant I was!

Now as I look back, I realize how overwhelming the entire scene must have been. From what I have been told, they had lived in Phoenix but had seen little and stayed indoors. The last two years living in rural Georgia was no preparation for Michigan Avenue on a summer day in June! I regret and am ashamed of how I reacted but believe that such experiences allowed them to know me better.

Over time, I became more willing to challenge their assumptions and beliefs. We had friendly and more animated arguments about religion, race, homosexuality, the death penalty, the infallibility of the Bible, and other topics that emerged. As we became friends, I shared my frustrations, dreams, failures, and successes with them, and in turn, they confided in me, and we built relationships that could withstand blowouts on Michigan Ave.

Certain events can help speed up the process, but rapport is commitment. And the task is much more complicated than Geertz suggests, especially when you are an white outsider working with a group that for two hundred years has placed white men on pedestals as emancipators and saviors. Moreover, rapport is something that is earned and takes a degree of humility.

An Unexpected Turn

As I noted in the introduction, the family's decision in the summer of 2012 to move to Des Moines, Iowa, was surprising and a blow to both my research and social life. Over the two years, the brothers and two other Karen families had become the center of both worlds. In the end, I decided to stay as involved in their life as much as I could via social media and annual visits.

Over the next two years, 2012 to 2014, I made annual trips from Georgia to Des Moines to visit them. Staying in their home gave me an even closer insight into their lived experiences and kept me up-to-date on the family's major life events. For example, in 2013, Sam Ber Htoo flew to Atlanta to visit his then fiancé Moo Paw (pseudonym) and asked if I would drive them to Des Moines so she could meet his family and receive their blessing. I flew back with Moo Paw and had a chance to talk with her and learn more about her Karen-American story and her hopes and fears for her future.

In 2015, as unexpectedly as when they notified me about moving to Iowa in 2012, they called to say they were returning to Sandville! It seems that Des Moines winters were tough on Brown and Esther.

Upon their return, they quickly bought a home in Sandville with money they pooled together. Since 2015, some or all the Htoos I worked with live on the other side of the Sandville, closer to Pineville, and have joined their local congregation. As of the writing of this manuscript, March 2022, Brown and Esther live with their two youngest children, Hser Ku and Ler Moo.

Notes

Epigraph: According to *Karen Proverbs*, this quote means, "Everyone is comfortable in their own place." Drum Publications, *Karen Proverbs*, 13.

1. Wilson and Singer, "Refugee Resettlement Metropolitan America."
2. Marshall, *Karen People*, 70.
3. Ferrars and Ferrars, *Burma*, 132.
4. Forbes, "Midwifery and Witchcraft," 266.
5. See Gilhooly et al., "Reading the Ink."
6. Geertz, *Interpretation of Cultures*, 416.
7. Geertz and his wife had only been in the village ten days when they accidently gained rapport.
8. Called *takraw* in Thai or *chinloon* in Burmese.

Chapter 4

Teaching, Confusing, and Collaborating

> We eat cucumber, we talk about the plant;
> we eat a bottle gourd we count its plant.
>
> —Karen proverb

In the summer of 2010, when I began teaching the Htoo brothers, I visited their home twice or three times per week. I first worked with high school brothers Sam Ber, Hser Gay, and Hser Ku.[1] The eldest brother, Moe Tha Wah, had dropped out of high school in Arizona when he turned eighteen, and although he was listed on my roster, he never joined our study sessions. Moe Tha Wah had started working at the poultry plant with his mother.

When we began our lessons, Sam Ber was nineteen years old and had just finished his senior year of high school. Since he had been unable to pass the Georgia High School Graduation Test (GHSGT), he would return to Sandville High School (pseudonym) in the fall of 2010 in the hope of passing the GHSGT. Hser Gay was seventeen years old and had just finished his junior year of high school (grade 11). Hser Ku Htoo was fourteen years old (soon to be fifteen) and had just finished his freshman year (grade 9) of high school.

We studied for two to three hours each visit. I then spent an hour working with the youngest Htoo brother, Ler Moo, who was ten years old and in the fourth grade. During our first summer together in 2010, my arrival for our study sessions was an event. All of the brothers would be waiting dutifully for me on the porch and eagerly greet me with notebooks in hand as I pulled up beside their house in my car. They would

Figure 4.1. Eating together (2019). © Daniel Gilhooly

help unload my car and assist me with my books, backpack, laptop, video camera, tripod, and other equipment. Within only a couple of visits, the brothers knew the routine and set up the tripod and camera without a word.

Each visit, I was served a plate of deep-fried egg seasoned with cumin (similar to egg foo young), a very hearty portion of long grain rice, some sliced cucumber, and a room temperature can of Mellow Yellow. Each meal I ate alone. I was always watched over devotedly by each of the brothers. If I dented the pile of rice, more was added. If I looked like I had finished my Mellow Yellow, another was immediately brought to me. As the novelty of my visits wore off, these meals were less grand and over time they became less frequent. Interestingly, after I was no longer the brothers' teacher, I was included in meals and ate side-by-side the brothers with Brown Htoo acting as my attentive host! (see figure 4.1.)

These meals reminded me so much of my experiences traveling in Southeast Asia. I was served with that same deferential treatment that had become familiar, and I can imagine those early American missionaries sitting down to similar meals two hundred years ago.

Teaching and Learning: Research and the Dialogic

Soon after I started teaching the Htoo brothers, I began reading the works of Paulo Freire in my graduate courses, and his philosophy of education became an inspiration for my work with the brothers. Freire's description of teaching and learning gave voice and direction to what I sought. Freire writes in *Pedagogy of the Oppressed* (2008):

> Through dialogue, the teacher-of-the-students and the students-of-the-teacher cease to exist and a new term emerges: teacher-student with students-teachers. The teacher is no longer merely the-one-who-teaches, but one who is himself taught in dialogue with the students, who in turn while being taught also teach. They become jointly responsible for a process in which all grow. In this process, arguments based on "authority" are no longer valid; in order to function, authority must be on the side of freedom, not *against* it. Here, no one teaches another, nor is anyone self-taught. People teach each other, mediated by the world, by the cognizable objects which in banking education are "owned" by the teacher.[2]

This is what I aspired to as a teacher and researcher. As someone learning about the Karen, I was well-positioned to learn from the family as a student. I would learn of their lives back in the camps, Karen culture and language, and their experiences in the United States. In turn, I was able to help them develop their English language repertoires and help them better navigate school. It seemed that both could be achieved simultaneously, as Freire suggests.

But there were obstacles to the type of relationship I aspired toward from the start. It was hard upholding my high ideals about the dialogic when two-thirds of my team was so unwilling to speak and preferred to defer to either their older brother or me with polite nods of acquiescence. The brothers had found a level of comfort in the banking system and had grown used to sitting in class and allowing teachers to make all the deposits.

Since they had already lived in the United States for more than two and a half years when we met, I was somewhat surprised by how unwilling the brothers were to speak with me, with the exception of Sam Ber. The tutor who worked with them in Phoenix in 2008, whom I met with and interviewed, shared with me how reticent all but Sam Ber were when she worked with them. And their English language learner (ELL) teacher in Sandville continually expressed her concern about their lack of willingness to speak in their ELL class. An early challenge was getting the brothers to speak. Over time, I realized that my role as a researcher proved a catalyst to dialogue.

One of the first resources I found about working with Karen students was the Karen American Communities Foundation (KACF) website. It provided tips about working with the Karen people that reinforced this idea of Karen deference toward whites. In a section called *Considerations for Individuals and Agencies Working with the Karen People of Burma in the United States: Do Not Depend on Karen People to Complain or Let You Know if They Have a Problem,* the anonymous author states:

> By virtue of being older, male, American, white etc. you are of higher status. A Karen person does not want you to lose face by complaining about your help or to be seen as ungrateful for the aid they are getting by complaining. We also worry about burdening you with requests. The word to describe this is "annade." "Annade" is best described as "I feel really bad that you have to go out of your way to do something for me." Furthermore, we feel we are at the mercy of those who know more. We do not want to antagonize or alienate the one person or resource that we depend on—for example, the caseworker.[3]

In manifold ways, each of the Htoos embodied *annade* and, while I do not see this characteristic unique to the Karen people, it was an issue in the early months working with them and a bridge I had to cross every time I met a new Karen person. For many Karen and other recent immigrants, a fear of inconveniencing precludes asking questions and seeking needed help and support from others about school, the health care system, the law, and other important topics. And without questions, it is difficult to teach effectively.

After reading the corpus of papers and books related to the American Christian missionary enterprise with the Karen people, I realized the depth and historical roots of this deference paid to whites. As described earlier, Karen attitudes toward whites were more than just deference, but a complex nexus of colonialism, Christianity, language, prophecies, war, and emancipation.

Having taught English in South Korea, I was familiar with the respect paid to teachers and found the brothers' shy politeness familiar ground. Yet, I wanted our studies and research collaboration to be a means of dismantling this passivity and deference. I saw our lessons and collaborations as the kind of problem-posing education promoted by Freire. Again, I defer to Freire.

> The students—no longer docile listeners—are now critical co-investigators in dialogue with the teacher. The teacher presents the material to the students for their consideration, and reconsiders her earlier considerations as the students express their own. The role of the problem-posing educator is to create, together with students, the conditions under which knowledge at the level of *doxa* is superseded by true knowledge at the level of the *logos*.[4]

This idea of problem-posing education was inspirational in how I taught and, later, during our collaborative research. But before any grand plans of following Freire, we had more immediate concerns.

Catching Up

I was initially given a packet of materials by the Migrant Consortium (my employer for the summer of 2010) filled with various worksheets. My job description was helping the brothers "catch up," as explained to me. Early on, I realized that worksheets and helping them "catch up" academically were difficult, if not impossible. They simply did not have their American peers' schema or the requisite English ability. But I stayed the course.

Sam Ber's and, to a lesser extent, Hser Gay's biggest immediate need was passing the GHSGT. In 2010, this exam decided who and who would not graduate from high school in Georgia. We spent months looking at sample questions and trying to make sense of it all. In total, Sam Ber Htoo and Hser Gay took the exam more than eight times, and although they became better guessers, it was clear that there was little possibility of ever passing all the subject areas without a degree of luck. It became clear that one of the biggest issues was their lack of understanding of the questions.

We decided to try first to understand what the questions meant and ways we could best make informed guesses. We worked on identifying keywords and trying to simplify the question. However, the pressures of this exam had two major drawbacks. First, the brothers placed so much importance on this exam that it became their sole motivator. Both brothers were so intent on the test that they all but stopped focusing on their class-work, and, more importantly, they saw little need to focus explicitly on their language development with me. They knew that receiving a diploma was important, which was their driving force to stay in school.

The second drawback of the test was that it contained so much information that the brothers had never formally studied. How can a student pass an examination covering the Civil War when they had little context of the periods before or after? As we studied, I soon realized they lacked so many contexts in all the content areas that I wondered how they had managed to pass any parts of the GHSGT. By their last attempt at the test both brothers were able to pass all the sections of the test except English Language Arts.

One particular lesson exemplifies the complexity at hand. We strug-gled through an hour on why "nineteenth century" was used to describe events in the 1800s. Sam Ber kept asking why the American Civil War was considered a nineteenth-century war when it happened in the 1860s. At first, I struggled to respond, and my explanations only confused the situation. After I got home and had time to think about things, I realized that making a timeline might help.

At our next meeting, I had them make a timeline at 1 AD until the present, 2010. The support helped Hser Gay and Hser Ku, but Sam Ber was still confused. Try as I might, I often left these lessons convinced that I had not only not taught them anything but that I had muddied the waters even more. There were just too many gaps in their knowledge and mine. I was a poor math student and unable to effectively teach math. In the end, I think creating visual aids like a timeline helped, but it was limited. With no prior exposure to Western history, scientific and mathematical concepts, and Western literature, they simply did not have the schema to catch up with their American peers.

However, my biggest mistakes early on were missing opportunities that connected the brothers to the content we were studying. For children of refugees, who fled a war-torn country, the topic of war would have been something they could have related to personally. These missed opportunities would have made the content more accessible. Over time, I became much savvier in making these explicit connections but early on, I missed opportunities to bridge their lived experiences with the topics we were studying. I, too, was caught up in the frenzy of passing the exam.

I felt we were making strides at times in their English speaking through our talks about all and sundry, but I was desperate to find something they could read and enjoy to help their reading and writing skills, which seemed paramount to passing the exam. It would also give them some important language experience apart from our lessons. Reading seemed critical for the short-term goal of passing the GHSGT and their long-term language development, academic success, and post-high school prospects. I started by looking at novels and short stories required in Georgia.

We spent months attempting to read condensed versions of these classic American short stories and novels. I would assign them a book to read that I had found at Goodwill, and each time, the book went unread. When I would rebuke them for not having read, they would shrug their shoulders, and that was it. I would scold them but with little effect. The brothers were uninterested and lacked the necessary vocabulary for any enjoyment, and book after book and reading after reading went unread. I then tried to use magazine articles to increase motivation, but inevitably, they fell short and also went unread.

I once brought them to the magazine rack at Wal-Mart and excitedly implored them to each pick out any magazine they wanted. After brief scrutiny of a few covers, they each walked away and said there was nothing they liked. I persisted, but only Hser Gay finally picked one, *Inked*, a tattoo magazine. I was disappointed the others had not selected anything but encouraged that at least one had selected something. On the drive home, I asked Hser Gay why he chose that particular magazine, and he said it was the only one with more pictures than writing!

An interesting anecdote with Sam Ber helped me better understand what they were experiencing and why nothing seemed to appeal to them. One day, I worked with a younger group of Karen kids at the Htoo house. Sam Ber came over to listen in on the lesson and started to leaf through one of the first-grade storybooks. Initially, he joked about reading a book intended for early grades children, but I soon noticed that he was not putting the book down and, rather, was reading more intently than I had ever observed. It was the first book I think he had ever read from cover to cover. It was also most likely the only book he had completely understood. When he put the book down, he was impressed with the story and himself. I became convinced that the problem was finding a book at their reading level that appealed to them. Sadly, I do not think we ever found that balance. However, I did stumble upon a book that caught their interest, and we were able to read it together.

The Book Little Daughter

In the spring of 2011, I found the autobiography *Little Daughter* (2009) by Karen author and activist Zoya Phan. I ordered a copy and began reading. Her story was much like the stories the Htoo family was sharing with me, and I decided that I had found a book that would interest them. Although it was beyond their reading level, I bought three more copies. I made a reading schedule and outlined my expectations for reading independently. They were instructed to highlight all new words but only use their dictionaries to check words that impeded their comprehension. They also had to keep a running list of new vocabulary with their own definitions.

They read independently for the first time. When we met, we reviewed vocabulary, read the text aloud, discussed the book, made connections between the author's experiences and their own, and finished up with a review of the vocabulary. This text choice worked in terms of motivating them to read but was above their reading level. We would often spend most of the lesson on one paragraph or page just going over problematic vocabulary. But it became a book that we started and finished together.

Ad Hoc Teaching and Learning

When I look back, read my field notes, and reflect on our study sessions, I realize that the most successful lessons were those that emanated naturally from our conversations before and after "lessons." Invariably, after our study sessions, the brothers, their older brother, parents, or a visiting friend or relative would be waiting for me to answer questions about a recent visit to the doctor, mail received, school notices, and other paperwork. In my attempts to explain, lesson ideas emerged. Over time I realized that these ad hoc lessons were serving as more meaningful lesson topics than when we "studied" more formally.

Whenever I saw their interest peaked about a particular topic, I tried to take advantage of the moment. This became a kind of improvisational teaching style based on their needs and interests. One set of lessons emerged while driving on the highway to visit some Karen relatives in Atlanta.

We all noticed a shiny red convertible sports car as we drove down the highway. It was clear the boys were star struck. Seeing how impressed they were, we began to talk about cars and their costs. I casually asked them what they thought such a car cost. After a long pause, Sam Ber, aged twenty at the time, exclaimed "one thousand dollars!" as if naming a price far beyond the actual value. That parlayed into a series of lessons on the cost and value of things from cars services to the price of a loaf of bread.

That week I brought over the Sunday newspaper as a resource. We went over the classifieds, talked about the cost of cars and apartments, and then tried to figure out the abbreviations. Grocery stores, sporting goods, department and hardware store inserts became literacy tools that they each responded to and took great interest in. They slowly began to realize the various costs of all and sundry. Other times, the brothers' gaps in knowledge were harder to fill and, therefore, harder to create lessons for but often led to interesting variations of perspective based on their schemas.

Some lessons were much more acute and affected their and their family's lives. One day the brothers told me how a cousin needed Sam Ber Htoo to accompany him to court to act as his interpreter. The cousin had been pulled over for expired registration and, since Sam Ber Htoo was the designated English speaker of his extended family, he would be accompanying the cousin as an interpreter. Though confident in his language ability, he was nervous about the prospect of speaking in a court of law. He had heard all sorts of stories about the US legal system and was justifiably worried about his responsibility. Like other immigrant communities, Karen people fear deportation, and it was clear that none of the brothers had any sense of how the justice system worked. This upcoming court date led to a series of classes focused on the language of the legal system and their rights under the law. These lessons were a means for them to consider broader issues related to citizens' rights while also gaining the requisite legal vocabulary. The brothers were each highly motivated to discuss and take notes on the various crimes, and they were equally enamored with all the punishments of the US legal system. In turn, they would share with me what they knew about Karen laws or rules.

Our conversations often led to interesting discussions and revelations about cultural similarities and differences. Sam Ber, in particular, liked to offer Karen perspectives of the world, and two stories in particular stick out to me as representative of the alternative cultural knowledge/perspective, knowledge/schema that students bring with them.

Schematic Mismatches: Waves and the Gift of Speech

In line with my commitment to experiential learning, I took the brothers on a field trip to Tybee Island just outside Savannah. It was their first trip to the ocean, and we made a weekend of it. The brothers came to my apartment on campus one Friday after school and delighted in free Internet and HBO. We woke at 2:00 a.m. and made the four-hour drive east. We reached the ocean just as the sun began to rise.

We spent the day walking the beach, body surfing, and enjoying a nearly deserted beach. Before leaving, we sat at the water's edge and watched as huge freighters lined up to disembark at the Port of Savannah. We were in awe of these massive ships as they grew larger and larger over the horizon. This led Sam Ber to expound on the source of the waves crashing at our feet. He explained how the mighty ships before us were the cause of the waves lapping our toes. "See how they make the waves," he exclaimed.

He talked about the waves he used to play in on the Moei River near the camps. He and his friends would wait for a longboat to pass by and then jump in the waves they created near shore. He reasoned that these ocean waves were bigger because the ships passing by were bigger. I commended his reasoning but had little more to offer, and we sat in silence. I half-heartedly attempted to explain that while boats do create waves, these waves were caused by the gravitational pull of the moon and sun, but in reality, I knew little about the causes of waves and tides. Sam Ber, unconvinced, laughed off my attempts to explain something he had witnessed with his own eyes. And to this day, I assume that when he sees a wave, he is looking for the boat that caused it. This was a lost opportunity for both of us to learn about the science of waves but does represent how schemas differ across cultures and individual experiences. These can be powerful teaching moments for culturally diverse students, teachers, and classmates.

Eating the Tongue of a Bird

Another story that speaks to the mismatch of schemas came soon after their brother Moe Tha Wah's wedding. In our first lesson after the wedding, I told the brothers how impressed I was with their father's ability to get the entire Karen community laughing during his wedding speech. Brown Htoo always could get the otherwise somber-looking Karen congregants of all ages and backgrounds to break into a smile or an outright burst of laughter. In their reactions and his tone, I surmised that his humor lay in his plain-spokenness. Sam Ber readily agreed with me about his father's talent, and the other brothers gave their usual silent agreement. Sam Ber then related to me the origins of his father's rhetorical perspicuity.

It seems that Brown's father always hoped that his son would become a great preacher. So, when Brown was just a boy, his father went into the jungle in search of a particularly melodious songbird who, it was believed, would bestow the gift of speech to anyone who ate its tongue. After downing the bird, he fed the tongue to Brown, who has had a golden tongue ever since. We all laughed, but I am certain that our laughter came from very different places.

School in Sandville

I visited them at school a few times and observed them in their ELL class. Based on what I was learning from their ELL teacher and what I observed, they rarely, if ever, spoke at school, on the bus, or at the few school events they attended. In interviews and our talks, they often reiterated their frustrations with school. I never formally tested them on listening comprehension, but it was clear that they understood the gist of what I was asking them the majority of the time. Sam Ber Htoo invariably took the lead and dominated the talk when we worked as a group. And, like many ELL teachers, I could have done a better job earlier on in finding ways to get the other brothers more involved. Over time I realized that the best way to get others talking was to work with them one-on-one. However, as they would tell me many times, this was not the case at school.

In school, they indicated understanding little or nothing of what their teachers were saying. In short, they were exposed to little in the way of comprehensible input provided by teachers, staff, and classmates.[5] It is hard to develop language, find any motivation, build language confidence, or view school as anything other than a necessary burden when you cannot understand your teacher. Like other language learners, the brother stopped trying to understand, picked up what they could, and stayed silent. Over time, they were uncharacteristically vocal about their frustrations with their classes and lack of comprehension. The usually stoic Hser Ku Htoo and Sam Ber Htoo described their experiences after the first day of the 2010–11 school year and summed up their collective feelings toward their schooling.

Hser Ku: Right now, I don't understand nothing. It's tough for me, that the end of the story.

Sam Ber Htoo: We have to go to school learning many other subjects. We have to do. But they don't have like a special school for learning only English. If you speak very well you can learn the other subjects, you know? Like about machine stuff, wire, welding like that, economics. You know it's hard learning economics, it not helping you a lot because you don't understand. You just teaching, learning that's why your English not very good.[6]

In fairness to their school, they represented more than half of the entire culturally and linguistically diverse (CLD) high school student population at the time. The school was woefully unprepared for the arrival of this little-known group from Burma. While some teachers seemed to be putting in the effort to meet their language needs, it appeared the brothers were treated with what could best be called benign neglect after the novelty of their arrival wore off. Each day, they had one pullout ELL class but otherwise sat beside their American peers in all other courses.

While their inability to understand their teachers was a major concern, what was most disconcerting about their education in Sandville was how few teachers even knew about or acknowledged their home culture and language. As late as 2011, after two years in the high school, some teachers thought they were Chinese, others Burmese, while others considered them Thai. I spoke with a parent in 2021 who was active with the Htoo family and other Karen families, and he argued emphatically that the family was from "Thailand." This misidentification of Karen students is common.[7]

Too often, Karen students are misidentified as Thai or Burmese. This is largely due to their paperwork, which usually indicates Burma or Thailand. The paperwork I originally received about the Htoo family and three other Karen families was confusing. For three of the families, under "Home Base Address," it indicated "Karen, TH," and under "country," it read "THI." And for the fourth family, it indicated "Burma." A teacher receiving such documentation would understandably be confused. And their confusion is only multiplied if they ask the students, "Where are you from, honey?" Any child I asked this question to or overheard being asked this question invariably answered "Thailand," even though they are not ethnically Thai, most often do not speak Thai, and only lived within the fences of a refugee camp in Thailand.

A teacher cannot tap into a students' home culture and language when they have not established where students are from, how they made it to your school, and what language they speak! Moreover, none of the schools in Sandville that catered to the growing Karen community had any professional development sessions related to working with this new and unique population. The brothers' frustrations with schooling became a major topic of discussion in many of our classes together and became a topic of interest during our collaborative research.

Teaching-Researching in the Home

My dual roles as teacher-researcher and the fact that I worked with the brothers in the intimacy of their home helped create more meaningful education. I had the time and space to ask questions, and they were more engaged listeners and speakers over time. Teaching in the Htoo home was also an effective means to listen to their personal and collective experiences. At home, the brothers were in a space where they felt comfortable and had more opportunities to express themselves about their experiences. For example, each of the brothers reported bullying to me but did not mention it to their teachers at school. Hser Ku Htoo expressed his anger toward one student bully.

> I hate that guy, man. Every day he makes fun at me in school. I don't like it man but I never say anything. He think he funny but I not laughing. I never know what he saying but I don't like it and some day I just tired. But I think it good I don't say nothing. I just want he stop. He crazy man.[8]

For a young guy who was already shy, experiences like this were affecting his language confidence. He was well aware of his classmates' smirks, which pushed him even more into silence. And the school seemingly did nothing. Yet, in the safety of his home, he was relaxed and more willing to speak. All the brothers became more talkative in our sessions as the weeks turned into months together.

The home was also an important setting for me to observe and experience their home environment, which gave me a sense of their roles in the family and their study habits. I was able to determine each of the brother's likes and dislikes and what they did for fun. I soon realized that their rural isolation was something they each had an opinion about that revealed something about them as individuals. Sam Ber Htoo liked the peace of rural life and was comfortable acting as the voice of the family at school, church, and with me. Hser Gay found their rural isolation boring and lonesome, and his escape was the social worlds of Facebook and talks via Oovoo with Karen across the diaspora. While Hser Ku and the youngest, Ler Moo, were happy with their rural isolation, Ler Moo had a best friend down the street, and Hser Ku was more comfortable with the laid-back vibe of rural living.

The home setting was also conducive to incorporating their home language and observing their home literacy practices. The brothers felt free

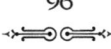
to use Sgaw Karen to help clarify for one another, which became a part of our lessons. And as I began to gain some insight into the Sgaw Karen language, this information helped me better recognize some of the negative transfer between English and Sgaw Karen that was affecting their English language development.

Sgaw Karen Language and in Home Literacy

As described in chapter one, the Sgaw Karen people had no orthography (written script) before the arrival of American missionaries. Like many Karen families, copies of the Sgaw Karen Bible were the only books in Karen homes in Sandville. Typically, each child has their own Bible. I am not a linguist, but I soon realized that a cursory look at their Sgaw Karen Bible and some consideration of the Sgaw Karen language revealed important differences between Sgaw Karen and English that served me as their teacher.

In Sgaw Karen writing, there are no breaks or spaces between words. Karen "sentences" are one string of letters, and a space is used only to end a sentence. This helped explain why all of the brothers demonstrated difficulties with the English spacing between words. I also noticed that all my Karen students struggled with English capitalization. This was most evident with the younger Karen kids I worked with but was evidenced in all three of the Htoo brothers' writing. When I realized that there is no capitalizing in Sgaw Karen, I was more aware of why both issues were prevalent.

Punctuation in English was also an early concern for the brothers, who demonstrated problematic punctuation in their writing. When I looked inside their Karen Bible, I soon realized that periods and commas are the only punctuation used.

Another feature of the Sgaw Karen language that was an issue for the brothers was the absence of verb tense. This was especially difficult for Sam Ber Htoo. Unlike his younger sibling, he was more connected to Sgaw Karen, and these mismatches with English were very difficult to overcome. Like most language learners, verb tenses, especially irregular verbs, were a persistent issue, but we could work on and discuss these as needed.

Pronunciation was also a language feature that I could focus on more acutely in the home environment. Unlike in school, where they rarely spoke, I had the chance to hear them speak, which enabled me to document and then address pronunciation issues. Sgaw Karen is monosyllabic; consequently, the brothers struggled with multisyllabic English words. And since Sgaw Karen has no final consonant sounds, I understood better why each of the brothers often dropped final consonants when speaking

English. Once I realized this difference, I could create activities that would target final consonants.

When we came across some of these mismatches between Sgaw Karen and English, we talked about language. These conversations are important in terms of teachers and students gaining metalinguistic awareness. I have been working with teachers in Kansas City schools for the past six years. One of the biggest issues I observe most frequently is the lack of language awareness of teachers who often struggle to put what they intuitively "know" about English into words so that their CLD students can understand why a certain language feature is used. Our talks about language were important aspects of our lessons that may not be possible in the school setting where teachers have multiple home languages at play and not enough time to digress into such conversations.

My Path from a Deficit to Asset Perspective

Like many teachers working with learners like the Htoo brothers, I initially felt that my job was about identifying their language needs and those areas where they needed to catch up. Too often, well-intentioned teachers become so wrapped up in identifying "needs" that they lose sight of the many assets these kids bring with them. I was ignoring or missing all of the assets the brothers brought to their school, our study sessions, and to their community and new country.

It was not until one of my meetings with my dissertation committee that I realized what I was doing. I was gently nudged to start considering the assets they each possessed. This was a transformative moment. I began to recognize and document these assets.

Once I started to take an asset perspective of each of the brothers, I began to create lessons that allowed them to use the skills they possessed. I began using more drawing in my classes in response to my observations of Sam Ber and Hser Gay's love of and ability in drawing. For example, I once asked the brothers to write a short essay about the differences between living in Phoenix and their lives in Sandville. They reluctantly wrote down a few opinions about both, but they were very much unmotivated. When I was packing up after the day's lesson, I offered the brothers some large easel pad paper I had brought along. In the moment, I decided to ask them to draw the same prompt about the similarities and differences between Phoenix and Sandville. When I returned for our next lesson, they presented their finished products.

Both their drawings were not only an expression of their skills as artists but revealed much about their life experiences (see figure 4.2). Sam Ber Htoo's drawing offers details about urban living that shocked me. One par-

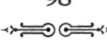

Figure 4.2. Detail of Sam Ber's drawing on life in urban America (2011). © Daniel Gilhooly

ticular detail revealed his growing racial prejudice. In a small urban street scene he drew, someone is shooting a gun with the caption, "Black man shoot Karen." This drawing prompted questions and led to conversations about his experiences living in urban Phoenix. I gained new insight into his experiences and the growing tensions between Karen and their black neighbors in urban areas. This led to discussions on race. Such conversations were possible because of my willingness to play to their assets and their willingness to talk about topics that they would never have addressed in school. These drawings could then be used to frame their writing.

Many days when I arrived for our lessons, Sam Ber Htoo and Hser Gay were practicing guitar. Assignments about music and musicians helped connect them to the content they found interesting. By simply sharing my laptop with Hser Gay, he created his own sounds on GarageBand.

These assets were not always related to a special skill or talent but an attitude or personality trait. I learned that Hser Ku was the family comedian and his dry humor kept the mood light. I doubt any of his teachers knew that he was so funny. I also realized that each brother longed for more socialization but had grown complacent in their attempts to mix with other kids at school. This led them to work in concert with their respective ELL teachers to find social opportunities.

ABAC and Extracurricular Activities

Sam Ber Htoo was the only brother to be involved in extracurricular activities in high school. He played off and on for the Junior Varsity soccer team. Otherwise, the brothers did not participate in any extracurricular activities that would have benefited them. In the early summer of 2011, their ELL teacher reached out to me with some applications for the brothers to join a two-week summer program sponsored by the Georgia Migrant Consortium. The program was a means to help migrant children learn more about college admissions and some of their options after finishing high school. It seemed a perfect opportunity for the brothers to socialize. She begged them to fill out the application form for weeks, but they resisted. As the brothers' spokesman, Sam Ber bore the responsibility to find an excuse to get them out of the program. But in the end, pressure at school and home led to Sam Ber and Hser Gay attending.

In 2011, we boarded a bus for Tifton, Georgia, and the Abraham Baldwin Agricultural College (ABAC). I came along as a chaperone for the bus trip and observed as the brothers mingled and met other participants in the program. Over the next two weeks, the brothers learned more about the possibility and process of attending college and met new friends. This experience was another transformative experience, and even Hser Gay came back with more English-speaking confidence.

In the end, what worked best were lessons and activities that responded to the brothers' interests and needs. I became a more effective teacher when I was flexible and willing to let topics emerge based on what the brothers were telling me about daily life and the responsibilities and demands in front of them. And it was also clear that the best learning was shared, dialogical, and inclusive of their cultural ways of knowing and understanding the world. The brothers learned differently and had different motivations, strengths, and limitations like all learners. This led to our collaborative research project in the summer of 2011.

Participatory Action Research: Our Collaboration

In 2010, I came across an article that described participatory action research (PAR) as a research method. I was intrigued, and the more I read, the more I began to imagine the possibilities for collaboration with the brothers. PAR is a research methodology that works in partnership with participant stakeholders. A key component of a PAR project is the call to action in response to the research data. We each found this appealing as we wanted to do research to make some difference. We began to consider ways to collaborate, and in the end, we decided to visit various Karen communities in the United States. We decided that we would have individual and collective goals for the project and began planning in the spring of 2011.

After each lesson, we started planning our trip. We decided to conduct our research in Des Moines, Iowa; Milwaukee, Wisconsin; and nearby Atlanta, Georgia. We chose these locations because of the brothers' access to friends and family in each city. The brother's maternal uncle hosted us in Milwaukee, and their sister Sar Ah and her husband hosted us in Des Moines. Since the brothers had many friends in Atlanta, it provided us access to the Karen in greater Atlanta.

We spent the spring busily preparing for our research-road trip. The brothers were instrumental in lining up interviews with friends and family. We devised questionnaires for both adults and adolescents, as I was most interested in comparing the brothers' experiences with schooling in rural Georgia to these more urban areas. We also devised interview questions, and we all practiced our interviewing techniques with friends of mine from my doctoral program. They also translated all our institutional review board (IRB) material into Sgaw Karen.

On 26 June 2011, we left Georgia equipped with video recorders, audio recorders, stacks of questionnaires, as well as a binder full of study material for the drive. Sam Ber Htoo and Hser Gay both had to take the GHSGT shortly after our return in mid-July, so I made photocopies of practice questions, timelines of US history, a list of the amendments to the Constitution, and a list of all US presidents. They became fun ways to pass the time while driving.

In each location, we were able to interview Karen youth and their parents about their experiences in school, the neighborhood, and work, and ask them about their hopes and dreams for the future. The brothers had lined up enough participants that our days were full. We spent time visiting various Karen homes and conducting individual and group interviews. And we always made time to answer any questions that participants had of us. In total, we spent two weeks between Iowa and Wisconsin and visited Atlanta periodically over the summer and into the fall of 2011. Those nights sleeping in Karen homes provided new insight into the early days of the Karen-American experience. I soon realized how lucky the Htoos and other Karen in Sandville were compared to Karen in these metropolitan areas.

I better understood the hostility toward blacks as in each community; we heard stories of fights and Karen kids getting jumped. We also witnessed the unsettling trend of Karen youth forming gangs for protection. It also taught me how limited an "insider" position I had outside of Sand-

Figure 4.3. Letter writing campaign (2012). © Daniel Gilhooly

ville. Many Karen in Des Moines and Milwaukee, where I had no insider status, looked at me with suspicion and fear until they realized I was "with" the Htoo brothers.

Upon our return, we sorted our data, discussed our findings, and began to consider ways to start addressing some of the issues we decided were most important. The brothers had used our research to find out more about other state graduation requirements. The brothers often talked with their friends and relatives about graduation policies in Iowa and Wisconsin and soon realized the Georgia graduation exam was unique. They were understandably indignant that they had to pass an exam that students in other states did not. We began thinking of ways we could address this issue, and I presented the idea of writing letters to the local superintendent and state education officials. Sam Ber Htoo and Hser Gay began a letter writing campaign to local and state education officials for three weeks (see figure 4.3)

While the campaign was intended to voice the brothers' indignation about state graduation requirements, it proved an excellent literacy project. In addition to gaining experience in the democratic process, the brothers gained skills in letter writing. It was the first time either brother had written a letter, so they gained experience in manifold ways, from address-ing envelopes, buying and attaching stamps, composing formal letters, and then dropping them off in a mailbox. They also gained experience developing their formal writing and realized the importance of writing multiple drafts and the hard work entailed in the writing process. They sent letters to the local superintendent of their county, the local congress-man, and the state superintendent of schools in Georgia. They received replies from each. This campaign was particularly successful because their writing became personal and purposeful.

Their congressman responded with a letter acknowledging their letter and referred them to education officials. Both superintendents responded with letters of appreciation and, more importantly, provided a path to receiving a waiver that would allow them to graduate without passing every section of the GHSGT. The pressure was on Sam Ber Htoo with only a few months before graduation and no possibility of returning to high school as he had already turned twenty-one.

No one at their school had informed them about the possibility of a waiver, and, though frustrated, we felt we had a possible course of action. We were able to access the requirements for this waiver and began apply-ing for waivers for both Hser Gay and Sam Ber. In the end, Sam Ber Htoo was denied a waiver and therefore could not graduate despite scoring higher than his brother in both math and English and only three points lower than Hser Gay in science. Hser Gay was granted a waiver and was able to graduate. It was devastating to Sam Ber, who, until the night before graduation, was expecting to walk for graduation. His name was even included in the graduation program besides his brother, but no one ever explained how or why he was denied.

Undeterred, all three brothers began taking action based on the new in-formation gleaned from our research collaboration. They shared informa-tion about the graduation exam and other information with Karen friends and new arrivals in Atlanta, where they were also enacting research in-dependent of me. They distributed questionnaires and conducted inter-views without my assistance, which added to our data. Moreover, the brothers began to self-advocate. Sam Ber Htoo successfully advocated for including Zoya Phan's book in the school's library collection to promote awareness of the Karen people locally. The success of their letter writing campaign led to another letter writing campaign to then Secretary of State Clinton before her trip to Burma. Importantly, their new identities as re-searchers led to their self-advocacy that elicited meaningful results, and we all learned the importance and potential of letter writing campaigns. It also demonstrated the efficacy of learning that is personal and self-directed. In 2015, Georgia Governor Nathan Deal signed House Bill 91 into law, ending the GHSGT. And importantly, the trip provided them an opportunity to speak in English and Sgaw Karen. Upon our return, I asked them each about what they had learned from the experience and Sam Ber Htoo and Hser Gay both indicated that they had learned new language.[9]

The height of Karen resettlement took place in 2011, and the brothers decided to make a list they shared with new arrivals to the United States. It was fascinating and eye-opening to read their suggestions. Hser Gay's list included the following:

1. Stop signs are very important. Read the sign before go forward.
2. You should learn all US sign before coming here.
3. If you drive more than 55–60 you will get a ticket by the police.
4. Be careful live in an apartment. Always lock the door, you might get kill or stole your money or value things.
5. In here a lot of Karen become gangster. Also, both boys and girls went the wrong way here [United States] smoking, drink, fight, wearing clothes [wearing gangster clothes].
6. Free to go to school.
7. You have to work hard here.
8. America is not very easy to live a long life. It is very difficult to live if you don't speak English.
9. If you miss more than 5 time at work you get fire—no more job for you.
10. Always ask help people when you need help. Don't be quiet and shy in the US, they will help you.
11. Money here is very expensive, it have big value.

Such lists were important discussion topics and opportunities to focus on specific language errors. Our research-road trip helped each of the brothers gain some language confidence. The once silent Hser Gay became much more willing to communicate. After our return, he applied for a driver's license and approached the clerk for the first time, and did not rely on either Sam Ber or me. He was able to negotiate the entire interaction at the DMV successfully. For the first time, he called customer service regarding his cell phone. His transformation speaks to the need to provide roles for language learners that help them develop language confidence, and smaller-scale collaborations can be a meaningful way for learners to engage in language. So many CLD students like the Htoo brothers lack opportunities to use their English and PAR projects of any size can be used for language development inside and outside schools.

Our collaborative research and studies were an important and effective means of teaching and learning, but each of the Htoo brothers' stories

is singular. Their personalities, ages upon arrival to the United States, schooling experiences in the camps and the United States, language proficiency, acculturation, and learning styles have shaped their American experience. Chapter 5 offers individual portraits of each of the four Htoo brothers.

Notes

Epigraph: According to *Karen Proverbs*, this Karen quote means, "Whatever we do, we should research it." Drum Publications, *Karen Proverbs*, 41.

1. I use their abbreviated names in this chapter as this is how I most often referred to them.
2. Freire, *Pedagogy of the Oppressed*, 89.
3. KACF, *Considerations for Working with Karen*. No longer available online.
4. Freire, *Pedagogy of the Oppressed*, 90.
5. See Krashen, "Bilingual Education," 63.
6. Conversation with Hser Ku and Sam Ber Htoo, Sandville, GA, 27 November 2010. Excerpt from discussion on schooling.
7. See "Karen American Communities Foundation."
8. Conversation with Hser Ku, Sandville, GA, August 2011.
9. Gilhooly et al., "Co-Creating the Dialogic."

Chapter 5

The Htoo Brothers

> All frogs are not fat, all fishes are not fat.
>
> —Karen proverb

One motivation behind this book is to share the individual experiences of four Sgaw Karen youth in their first years in the United States. By doing so, teachers can better understand each of the brother's experiences with school and their lives after graduating or dropping out of school. The Htoo brother's experience also helps demonstrate how their schools and I have contributed to their academic successes and failures. We start with the eldest Htoo brother, Moe Tha Wah.

Moe Tha Wah: The Elder Brother

Moe Tha Wah (Life Gold White) was a peripheral figure throughout my work with the Htoo family, but his story is worth telling as it speaks to the experiences of others who resettle during adolescence. Moe Tha Wah arrived in the United States two months before turning eighteen. I never worked directly with him as a tutor and have only interacted with him a handful of times over the past ten years. However, I always made a point to keep abreast of his life over the years.

By my arrival in 2010, he worked the second shift at a poultry plant six days a week alongside his mother, Esther. He was usually sleeping or had already left for work when I arrived. Most of his free time was spent near Atlanta with Karen friends. When we did interact, it was usually to help him with paperwork from work or related to his cell phone.

Moe Tha Wah's story is emblematic of many immigrants and refugees who arrive in their later teens. He represents what Rubén G. Rumbaut refers to as a 1.25 generation immigrant,[1] sharing most characteristics of his first-generation immigrant parents. Like Brown and Esther, his struggles with language have continued well beyond his school years and have placed limits on him compared to his younger siblings.

When the family first arrived in Phoenix, Moe Tha Wah was only two months shy of his eighteenth birthday and joined his brothers Sam Ber and Hser Gay at Central High School. He attended high school until the end of the 2007–8 school year before dropping out. He decided it was too much to catch up and decided to join Job Corps. He trained to be a security guard. Moe never worked in Phoenix because he joined his father to help the family get established in Sandville. In those early days in Sandville, before the rest of the family joined them, Moe Tha Wah and his dad worked first harvesting and then planting sunflowers.

After six months, he joined his cousins and mother and took a job deboning chickens at a chicken processing facility nearby. The plant was an early magnet for the growing Karen population in Georgia. More than a hundred Karen men and women commuted from Sandville and as far away as Atlanta, an hour drive away. At the plant, he met other young Karen and soon spent his free time with Karen friends in Clarkston, Georgia.

After fourteen months working at the poultry plant and commuting with his older cousins, he had saved enough money for a car. However, his limited English proficiency kept him from applying for a license in Georgia. So, he and his cousin returned to Phoenix, where he knew someone to help him take the driver's test in the Karen language. Interestingly, multiple adults made this twenty-six-hour drive back to Phoenix in those early days to attain their licenses. When I asked him why he went so far away to take the test, he said it was "easy" in Arizona. It speaks to the policy differences in states when it comes to state bureaucratic systems like the DMV. For whatever reason, the Arizona Department of Transportation has a Karen language driver's license manual that he used to prepare for the test.

As the only driver in the family at the time, Moe Tha Wah became responsible for much of the family's transportation needs. But with mobility, he became increasingly independent. The family relied on Esther's income and their funds through the Supplemental Nutrition Assistance Program (SNAP). According to his brothers, he saved and spent his money like many others in their late teens and early twenties, partying with Atlanta friends and gaining a liking for cards and beer.

Moe Tha Wah's trips to Atlanta led to meeting Paw Lwe (pseudonym), a sixteen-year-old Pwo Karen high school student living with her mother and sister in Clarkston, Georgia. After a six-month courtship, Moe Tha Wah sought the blessing of his parents to marry. His engagement was met with some apprehension, as Paw Lwe was Buddhist. Brown and Esther decided that they would reluctantly consent if she were willing to convert to Christianity. Brown and Esther also seemed to think that their future daughter-in-law was too young to marry. Three weeks later, on 5 October 2011, she was baptized at Sandville Baptist Church, and on 13 November 2011, they were married at Sandville Baptist Church across the street from the Htoo home. Like many Karen weddings in the United States, Karen attendees came from towns and cities across the southeast and beyond. Local congregants also attended with Pastor Rus presiding.

Before their wedding, Paw Lwe dropped out of the tenth grade of high school and remained with her mother a few weeks after the wedding before settling in with the Htoos. Though she lived in the home where I was a frequent visitor, she never engaged with me directly and was rarely seen. The brothers often jokingly called her "the shadow."

Moe Tha Wah and his wife lived with the family in Sandville for nearly six months before he quit his job at the poultry plant and announced he had decided to move to Des Moines, Iowa. He and his new wife chose to live with his sister Sar Ah and her husband and small child. Paw Lwe returned to live with her mother in Clarkston, Georgia, while he settled in and found a job. As explained to me later, Sar Ah, the eldest Htoo child, was trying to bring her family to Iowa, where she said there were more job opportunities and where she planned to buy a home for her entire family. Moe Tha Wah jumped at the chance for a fresh start. He started work soon after arriving, and a few months later, he was reunited with his wife and newborn son.

Moe Tha Wah has been unsettled in the United States. He has moved repeatedly between Georgia and Iowa, ostensibly for better employment opportunities. He often expressed some dissatisfaction with his life in the United States and growing tensions with his wife. They had another son in 2015 but separated soon after.

In 2020, Moe Tha Wah decided to return to Thailand to live with someone he met on Facebook. He planned to start anew and use the money he saved to get established. Since he had not become a US citizen and, therefore, never was able to attain a passport, he had to apply for a permanent resident travel document, which allowed him to travel outside the United States for up to one year, but Moe Tha Wah had no intention of returning to the United States.

He took his savings but still contributed money toward buying Brown and Esther's house in Sandville, and departed for Thailand. After three months in Thailand, he returned to the United States and moved in with his parents in Sandville with little idea of future plans. A few weeks after his return I visited the family. He looked unhealthy and withdrawn when

Figure 5.1. The Htoo brothers and the author (2012). © Daniel Gilhooly

I met him. He also seemed to be carrying a heavy mental burden of worry and concern about his children's welfare and his own standing with the law. Moe Tha Wah shared a letter from the Iowa Department of Family Services notifying him that his wife had lost custody of the children and that they had been placed with his mother-in-law back in Georgia. He asked me to review these documents and advise him on how he should respond. I told him he should contact the Iowa Department of Family Services if he wanted custody of his children. I also told him that he should visit his children since they were nearby and make sure he had a job and was settled before any efforts at custody. He gave no discernible sign that he would follow my advice and I left it that.

After returning to the United States, he stayed with Brown, Esther, and his brothers. For the next six months, he never sought employment and rarely left his parents' house. According to his brothers, he slept all day and was sick. The family was justifiably worried about his mental and physical health, and he had no health insurance. He indicated that he has asthma, preventing him from working. However, I think other reasons may influence him to remain so withdrawn. A story that swept through the Karen community may have played a part in his fears.

As it was related to me through a few Karen sources, the story has become a cautionary tale for many Karen men. Around 2014, a Karen couple were divorced, and the wife took custody of their eight children and soon began living with an American man. The husband was not paying child support, and over time his wages began to be garnished. He fled to Virginia to work, but his wages were garnished again. According to the story related to me, the man was so distraught that he killed himself. This and other cautionary tales may play some part in why Moe Tha Wah was reluctant to work again, but this is only conjecture.

It has been expressed to me multiple times by the Htoo brothers and other Karen that many Karen men are fearful of divorce because of having to pay child support. And as far as I can tell, based on my continuing work in Sandville, separations of young couples like Moe Tha Wah and his wife are becoming more and more common. In any tight-knit community, rumors and anecdotes metastasize, leaving many fearful of the unknown. Whatever the reason, Moe is living in fear and confusion about how to proceed with his life and what role he can play in his children's lives. In 2021, Moe moved back to Iowa and is now working and living at his sister Sar Ah's house in Des Moines.

Throughout my years teaching the Htoo brothers, I worked closest with Sam Ber Htoo (aka Sam Ber), Hser Gay Htoo (aka Narko and later Sedan Htoo), Hser Ku Htoo, (aka Gola), and the youngest, Ler Moo.

Like their older brother Moe Tha Wah, Sam Ber Htoo and Hser Gay Htoo are considered 1.25 generation immigrants as they arrived in the United States between the ages of twelve and seventeen.[2] However, Sam Ber was seventeen upon arrival, and Hser Gay was fifteen, and they each had the benefit of a few years of schooling before facing the realities of adulthood.

Hser Ku Htoo, the second youngest, is considered a 1.5 generation immigrant as he arrived in the United States when he was ten years old.[3] Ler Moo, the youngest of the brothers, is considered a 1.75 generation immigrant since he came to the United States at age seven. Because he came so young, he inhabits a middle space between the host culture and home culture.[4] However, unlike many 1.5 or 1.25 immigrants, none of the brothers have had any direct experience with their homeland, Burma. Therefore, they are not altogether typical 1.5 or 1.25 generationers but share some characteristics of second-generation immigrants "for whom the homeland mainly exists as a representation consisting of parental memories and memorabilia."[5]

The experiences of these four brothers, who came to the United States at different ages and had different experiences with schooling, language learning, and socializing reflect the challenges faced by other immigrant and refugee background children. Moreover, as well shall see, in the case of the youngest brother, Ler Moo, challenges are faced by even those children that resettle at very young ages. The two youngest, Hser Ku and Ler Moo knew less about the Karen insurgency, Karen history and language, and Karen cultural practices than their older brothers. They were also far less political than their brothers, and camp life's hardships seemed a vague memory.

Sam Ber Htoo

I begin with a short autobiographical essay Sam Ber wrote as a homework assignment after our first meeting, 1 May 2010 (age nineteen):

> My name is Sam Ber Htoo. I was born in Thailand. I speak Karen language. I have four brothers and one sister. I am 3rd person. I live in Thai mae la refugee camp. A lot of people live in Thai mae la refugee camp. I went to school when I was seven years old. It's very hard to go to the school. You have to pay money for school. It's really hard to find money in the camp. You can't allow to go outside the camp. If you go outside the camp, the police will catch you Because I don't have a picture card I saw many people escaped to find money outside the camp. Some people went to Bangkok and border of Burma to find money. I live in Thailand 17 year. It's was really hard to live in the camp.
>
> Then, I never know and I never thought I came to America I heard the government say, if you want to go to America, you can apply to go. Then you have to introduce about yourself. After that, we pass everything about the Question. Then I came to American when, September 7, 2007 in Phoenix, Az. I live in Arizona one year. Then I came moving to Georgia. I like here better than when I lived in Thailand. I very happy to be with my family and the other people. I thought God planned wonderful for us.

Sam Ber Htoo, like many Karen, goes by the nickname Chit Poe (Little One) because of his diminutive frame. He is the third child of Brown and Esther. Sam Ber was sixteen years old upon resettlement to the United States. When we first met, he was nineteen years old and had just completed his junior year. He can read, speak, and write Sgaw Karen and English. In 2018, he began informally learning to speak Burmese from a Burmese-speaking coworker. His name Sam Ber was intended to be December, his birth month.

Sam Ber was born in Bornho Refugee Camp (now defunct) in 1990, shortly after his parents' flight from Burma. He lived most of his life in Mae La Refugee Camp, where he attended school until eighth grade. According to his transcripts, when he arrived in Phoenix, he was placed in the ninth grade at Central High School. He advanced to the tenth grade

Figure 5.2. Sam Ber Htoo (2012). © Daniel Gilhooly

the following school year (2008–9). In the summer of 2008, he took an En-glish language class to help develop his English language proficiency. He also had an English language tutor. In Phoenix, he established his role in the family as its spokesperson. He worked and built a relationship with the family caseworker and managed the family's affairs.

When he arrived in Sandville, Sam Ber was placed in the tenth grade. Therefore, he was moved along the normal grade trajectory despite lim-itations in all English language domains. After our first lesson, my first impressions of Sam Ber are reflected in the following field note entry.

> Sam Ber's willingness and desire to speak English bodes well for his future development. Although his writing is competent, he needs to work on gram-mar, punctuation, and capitalization and develop academic vocabulary. Sam Ber would benefit from SAT preparation in anticipation of taking the exam [at the time; I misunderstood which exam he was studying for. He studied for the Georgia High School Graduation Test (GHSGT), not the SAT]. He was the only one to speak with me today and expressed an interest in sports, music, and movies. He suggested I watch Rambo IV as it is his favorite movie and about the Karen.[6]

Sam Ber was easy-going and always ready to talk and ask questions during our study sessions. He was one of the few Karen I met of his generation that asked questions and sought help from teachers, neighbors, and congregants from Sandville Baptist. He also demonstrates the best Sgaw Karen language skills of each of the brothers and writes the Sgaw Karen script beautifully.

I was surprised in the spring of 2011 when we received his World-Class Instructional Design and Assessment (WIDA) ACCESS scores. His overall WIDA core was 375 out of 600 (proficiency score of 3.1 out of 6). While his grammar, writing, and listening scores matched my own assessment he, surprisingly, scored the lowest among his brothers in speaking, with a score of 337 out of 600 (2.4 out of 6), which places him at the high end of the beginner level. While his grammar and word choice were flawed in my assessment, his willingness to speak in English set him apart from his siblings and most other Karen I have worked with over the years. For me, this score speaks more to the fallibility of the WIDA exam or its administration. Or maybe he was having an off day. Sadly, WIDA does not consider factors such as waking at 5:00 a.m. to catch a bus and a school that proved less than receptive to their CLD students. Although the state of Georgia had been using WIDA since 2005, the brothers were never tested until two years after their arrival.

Despite his diminutive frame, Sam Ber is an excellent athlete. He is known nationally within the Karen diaspora community and other Southeast Asian communities for his skill in cane ball. In summers, he and his teammates travel to all corners of the country, playing in these lucrative tournaments. He is also a very talented soccer player and played one season for his high school junior varsity soccer team. He plays soccer as an adult on various Karen church teams that often play in regional and national tournaments for substantial cash prizes. We often played soccer, basketball, and countless matches of cane ball, all of which he demonstrated his athleticism.

Like many Karen men, Sam Ber is a self-taught guitarist who enjoys writing and singing love songs and Christian ballads. He is very interested in Karen history, proverbs, and myths. He was an excellent source of information about Sgaw Karen culture and a storehouse of fascinating details passed down from his father, aunts, and uncles. He plans on teaching his children these stories. He is also an excellent artist and demonstrated his drawing skills in school and in our study sessions.

Despite poverty, his difficulties in school, and his lack of friends, Sam Ber was always remarkably upbeat and rarely had a discouraging word about life in the refugee camps, his struggles in the United States, or the many obstacles he faced in school and life. However, he was very vocal about his frustrations with schooling in the United States and very critical of the Georgia education system.

As noted earlier, Sam Ber took and failed the GHSGT multiple times. While his brother received a waiver for the exam, Sam Ber was denied the same waiver. He was noticeably upset with the state's decision not to grant him a waiver and, therefore, not graduate high school after attending for three years with perfect attendance. He participated in the graduation ceremony to support his brother and handled the situation with great poise and maturity. It was particularly excruciating seeing his name listed in the commencement program. Sadly, because the family moved to Iowa only a few days after graduation, we could not determine why he was not afforded the same waiver given his younger brother.

Sam Ber is an active Christian and a Karen nationalist, as he believes in the Karen cause of establishing an independent Karen state. He often expresses his religious beliefs on Facebook and in conversation and his support for the KNU's sixty-year insurgency against the Burmese Army. He often expresses his Karen pride by wearing traditional Karen clothing and always carries a traditional Karen-style bag. He frequently wears a T-shirt with the image of the Sgaw Karen independence leader and British-educated KNU founder, Saw Baw Oo Gyi. Sam Ber regularly spoke about his desire to return to Thailand to help at the refugee camps.

Compared to other Karen who arrived in the United States as adolescents, Sam Ber was outgoing and talkative outside his Karen community. Many of his Karen peers that I have met tended to be more passive and reticent. In contrast, Sam Ber aligned himself with American "helpers" and was less reluctant to ask for help, and, equally importantly, he maintained these relationships. He maintained relationships with his first English tutor in Phoenix and his caseworker from Arizona. In Sandville, he often turned to me, the pastor at Sandville Baptist, his ELL teacher, or willing congregation members to procure information and services, read mail, make phone calls, and find solutions to all and sundry.

Only days after completing his senior year, Sam Ber moved with his family to Des Moines, Iowa, to reunite with his sister and brother-in-law. Before he left, I interviewed him about the prospects of moving to Iowa and his plans after high school. He was twenty-one years old, and I had not heard him talk about what he might do now that he was no longer eligible to continue high school in Iowa. He replied without hesitation, "I want to get fat and sleep." At the time, I was stunned by the response and was quick to judge. Today, I am ashamed of my response and think I better understand what he meant.

Sam Ber had tried at high school in Phoenix and Sandville without a diploma, and he was tired and frustrated. He awoke every morning at 5:30 a.m. to catch the bus and did not return home until 4:00 p.m. He maintained perfect attendance throughout his schooling in Sandville. It was no wonder he wanted to sleep. He was a skinny young guy who tried to buff up and put on some weight. But my American self, who puts so much weight on one's "work ethic," could not help but judge. And, I was later to find out, I was not alone. One of his American helpers had lined up a part-time job for him at a Japanese restaurant, but he told her he "needed to rest." It did not go over well.

In hindsight, given better proficiency in English, he might have been able to express his frustration and exhaustion and his need to take a break for a while. But he did not or could not, and so misunderstandings and miscommunications led to judgment. But he did not or could not say this, and such misunderstandings only add fodder to those who think immigrants and refugees only come to the United States to sleep and get fat off taxpaying Americans.

I think of Sam Ber often when I read some of my students' papers. As a university professor who prepares my pre-service teachers to work with CLD students, I assign all my courses a project called "My American Story," which asks students to reflect on their family's American experience and core beliefs and values. And after reading hundreds of these over the past six years, it is clear that "hard work" is our primary virtue. So I reacted as I did and thought him lazy and unmotivated. From my perspective, I saw a family in need of as many paychecks as possible and judged him as a freeloader unwilling to meet his responsibilities. Today, when I look back on the past eight intervening years, I empathize with him. He was the sole driver in the family and had many responsibilities at home. He was rightfully tired and in need of a break. I see why he was less than anxious to begin working, and I chastise myself for my insensitivity. But at the time, I only heard those damning words, "I want to get fat and sleep," and I made it clear that I found his response far from acceptable.

Des Moines and a New Start

After eight months in Des Moines, Sam Ber got restless and started his first job. He worked for an envelope manufacturer or distributor for six months and then quit. Upon visiting Des Moines in 2013, he talked of his job and why he decided to leave. He complained of his schedule, labor conditions, little pay, and the unfair treatment by his Vietnamese supervisor. He also wanted to return to school to attain his adult high school diploma.[7] He returned to community college and received an Adult High School Diploma in 2013.

While conducting interviews for our collaborative research in 2011, Sam Ber interviewed a newly resettled Sgaw Karen girl, Moo Paw (pseudonym), in Clarkston, Georgia. They kept up a friendship via social media and later by cell phone when he moved to Iowa. In the summer of 2014, with the consent of his parents, Sam Ber returned to Georgia to be closer to Moo Paw and lived with friends in an apartment complex in Clarkston. He quickly found employment at a bathroom fixtures manufacturer polishing faucets. Soon after, he and Moo Paw married in Clarkston and Brown came down from Iowa. It was a beautiful ceremony, and I was excited and happy for them.

Before his marriage, I had the chance to drive Sam Ber and Moo Paw from Atlanta to Iowa to meet Brown and Esther. Moo Paw was nervous, but it was clear she was the more mature of the two. She had grown up fast. She was responsible for managing her family's affairs since arriving in the United States. Sam Ber was giddier and in love, while Moo Paw was more reserved but seemingly happy with his affections. Sam Ber and Moo Paw sat snuggled in the back seat while I drove the fifteen hours north. We stopped in Saint Louis to see the arch and admire the Mississippi River, and while taking pictures, I remember watching them and wondering what was in store for them.

After spending two days with Sam Ber's family, Moo Paw and I flew back to Atlanta. We had a chance to talk, and I found her to be hard-working, ambitious, and realistic as she spoke about the prospects of attending community college and finding a career. She was uncertain about what lay ahead but appeared more grounded than Sam Ber. She also spoke of the challenges she had faced since arriving in the United States and her current job.

Moo Paw had arrived in the United States in 2012 and was responsible for her younger sister and her ailing parents. Her father had been diagnosed with diabetes and was receiving dialysis and was unable to continue working at the poultry processing plant. Her mother was also unemployed, spoke no English, and was frail and in poor health. Her younger sister was in middle school and too young to help out financially. Moo Paw worked as a waitress at a French restaurant and hoped to attend community college even though she had not received a high school diploma. She seemed overwhelmed but driven.

After marrying, Sam Ber moved in with his in-laws in a two-bedroom apartment in Clarkston. They had two boys: Christ Ler (Christ Life) was born in 2015, and Stephen Htoo was born the following year. He named his eldest as an expression of his faith and chose Stephen in honor of the guitarist Stevie Ray Vaughn, whom Sam Ber has always admired. For some reason, Stevie Ray Vaughn and Christ seemed to be the perfect pair of names for Sam Ber's kids.

Sam Ber was the only breadwinner for most of time between 2014 and 2019, with Moo Paw working periodically. While Moo Paw's mother helped take care of the children, her father was dependent on their daughter and Sam Ber for transportation to dialysis, interpreting at the doctor's office, and monitoring his diet and medicines. I only visited the family apartment four times, and other than cramped quarters, the family seemed content. I remember one funny incident when Sam Ber returned to Sandville to buy some hens from his aunt. He casually tied them together by the feet and put them in a box on the back seat of my car. When I asked him where he would keep them in their tiny urban apartment, he responded, "In the apartment." Silly me.

In the spring of 2019, Moo Paw unexpectedly filed for divorce with little explanation other than that she wanted a clean break from her previous life. A dumbfounded and disconsolate Sam Ber was at a loss. It seems she left with no more than a bagful of clothes and many unanswered questions. She had no contact with Sam Ber until she announced the date of their court appearance. The couple was divorced in 2019 after five years of marriage.

Sam Ber moved back with his parents in Sandville with his two boys, staying through the summer of 2019. Equally surprising as his divorce from Moo Paw was a call I received from Sam Ber in the fall of 2019, a month after the legal proceedings. He announced that he had relocated to Omaha, Nebraska, to live with a Karen woman who was in a similar situation with two kids of her own. Their online relationship led to his decision to return to the Midwest. Omaha, Nebraska, is home to one of the largest Karen communities in the United States.

Sam Ber took care of his and his new girlfriend's two children while she worked as a waitress at a local Thai restaurant. Then in February 2020, they all moved to Des Moines, Iowa, to live with his sister Sar Ah and her family. Sam Ber started work at his old job sorting envelopes, but that job was cut short by the COVID-19 pandemic. He quit out of fear as so many Karen working in various factories were contracting the virus. In the summer of 2020, they returned to Omaha after visiting her parents in Ohio and then had a weeklong stay with his family back in Georgia. Shortly after their return to Omaha, he called me again to notify me that he was back in Des Moines with his kids and no longer in a relationship.

Hser Gay Htoo

Hser Gay Htoo wrote the following autobiographical short essay during our first lesson:

Figure 5.3. Hser Gay Htoo (2012). © Daniel Gilhooly

My name is Hser Gray. I was born in Thailand. I had lived in Thai Refugee camp For along times. There is nothing change in my life. When I was a kid my parents sent me to school. I was happy that I have met nice teachers and many good Friends.

I'm boring in the camp and we have no way to go out of the gate. All my feel is, this is very hard life in a long time in the camp.

After I was born in Thai border came new place. Than because of Burmese soldier conquer us and for our village so my parents move us Mae la camp. When I arrive in Mae la camp I went to school. I have met good friends and I play, studied and I have alot of fun. OPE [Overseas Processing Entity] opened the way to go to US so we came move United States. I had took a plane to Phoenix, AZ and I have go to school. My school names Central High School. I had made alot friends. I have live about 1 year in Az, after than I know and go to Georgia. I go to church every Sunday, have good neighborhood. I never I live is gonna be like this.

Hser Gay Htoo (Sweet Good Gold), also known as Narko and then Sedan, was born in Tah Lah Thaw Refugee Camp, Thailand, in November 1992. In his biography, he wrote his name as Hser Gray and not Hser Gay as on his official documentation. Early on, he learned the price one pays to have the name Gay, so he always referred to himself as Hser Gray and then went by the nickname Narko. His name means Sweet Good Gold.

He attended school in Mae La Refugee Camp until 2006 when he moved to a Christian boarding school outside the camp, which he pursued independent from his parents to receive a better education. I imagine that someone recognized his intelligence, and he was rewarded with an offer to attend a better school outside the camp.

He was fifteen years old upon resettlement in Phoenix and seventeen years old when we first met. He can read, speak, and write Sgaw Karen and English. My first account of Hser Gay reads as follows:

> Comments: Hser Gay lacks confidence when speaking English. His listening comprehension and writing are good. However, his limited vocabulary limits his ability to communicate. He demonstrates knowledge of many grammar structures but still needs improvement in word choice and verb tenses. His most pressing need is improved pronunciation and confidence. He also needs to increase his volume; he mumbles. I had major difficulties understanding his responses, and he is notably shy.[8]

When Hser Gay arrived in Phoenix, he was placed in the ninth grade with Sam Ber. And, like Sam Ber, he was also placed in the tenth grade upon arriving in Georgia in January 2009. Hser Gay took the GHSGT more than eight times. He eventually passed each of the exam sections except for English Language Arts (ELA). Despite failing the ELA section of the exam, he was granted a hardship waiver from the State Board of Education after conducting the letter-writing campaign described earlier. In May 2012, he graduated from Sandville High School with a 100 percent attendance record and an 84 percent overall GPA.[9] He was the first within the Karen community in Sandville to graduate from high school.

In 2011, he took the World-Class Instructional Design and Assessment (WIDA), and his scores were a surprise. He scored 428 out of 600 (a proficiency score of 6 out of 6) on speaking, the highest level, and his overall score was 398 (a proficiency score of 4.2 out of 6). His lowest score was on listening 2.5, which does not match my assessment of him. His reading score was another surprise as he scored a 401 out of 600 (a proficiency score of 5.6 out of 6), again placing him in the highest level despite not being a very active reader.

Hser Gay was so shy for the first months I worked with the brothers that he never spoke above an incoherent murmur and was wont to look down at his shoes rather than at me. He would smile sheepishly but rarely repeated himself if asked to repeat something. If I brought over a friend from university, he was even more reticent. Nevertheless, his English-speaking ability developed the most of all the brothers over time. By the end of our collaboration, he was more willing to speak in

English and demonstrated the widest language repertoire of anyone in the family.

Hser Hgay seemed to transform the most due to our research trip and studies. After our research collaboration, he expressed new confidence in English and as a researcher. In addition to being the first in his family, and the Karen community in Sandville, to graduate from high school, Hser Gay continually demonstrated himself to be an intelligent and, over time, an opinionated young man. He often complained about his schooling, life in the United States, his disdain for their rural isolation, and often expressed a wish to return to Thailand. Like his older brother, he shared in their father's mistrust of the Burmese and supported the insurgency efforts of the KNU. And back in 2011, he expressed a wish to return to Burma to join the fighting or start a business.

Hser Gay is an ingenious builder, musician, and self-taught master of the computer. He spent many afternoons building and creating things digitally and with whatever materials he could find. He was fond of making rings out of US coins for a time, namely quarters. A process involving a rusted metal spike and a dumbbell used as a hammer. He also liked writing and recording his music and patiently figuring out video editing software. He is also a self-taught guitarist. He spent many hours each day and late into the night chatting with new and old friends alike via his laptop computer. He expressed an interest in becoming a mechanic, translator, or businessman in high school.

Hser Gay became more independent and relied less on his older brother Sam Ber to speak for him. I often sensed he was holding back from contributing to our conversations due to his deference to his older brother. But by 2012, he was able to procure his own driver's license, disconnect the family's Internet service by phone, and order his food when we went out to a restaurant together. Frankly, these seemed like unrealistic goals only two years prior when we first met. Hser Gay was the only brother who eventually did not defer to Sam Ber and, over time, began to take on more of the family responsibilities.

Des Moines

Like his older brother, he worked for six months at a factory job after moving to Iowa but quit to find something more to his liking. In March 2013, he found employment at a coffee factory in Des Moines and expressed satisfaction with the work and salary. He was learning how to operate heavy equipment, and it seemed that he had found his calling. In my interviews with him on my visits to Iowa, it was clear that he was becoming more independent and spending more time away from home.

When his older brother Sam Ber moved back to Georgia to stay closer to Moo Paw in 2014, Hser Gay took on more family responsibilities. He became the family interpreter and provided transportation for his parents and younger siblings. However, in an interview shortly after his brother's move back to Georgia, Hser Gay expressed frustration with the added responsibilities and began staying at home less frequently, opting to stay at friends' houses instead and drinking beer with friends regularly. An interview with his younger brother Hser Ku in the summer of 2014 foretold Hser Gay's legal woes. Hser Ku expressed concern about Hser Gay's increased drinking and unwillingness to help at home. I barely had a chance to see him on my visit to Iowa in the summer of 2014. Promises to meet me for a talk would never materialize, and it was clear he had a life outside of work. I was disappointed that we never got a chance to talk but was happy for him.

In late 2014, Hser Gay was arrested for OWI (operating while intoxicated), and later a warrant was posted for his arrest for not showing up at his court date. It seems he understood little of the court proceedings and had missed his court date due to a miscommunication. His driver's license was suspended, and he paid a hefty fine.

Due to his legal issues, he could not join the family upon their return to Georgia in 2014. Since his license had been revoked, he found it hard to maintain his job. He would join the family in Georgia in spring 2016. Upon returning to Georgia, he worked at the local poultry plant with his younger brother Hser Ku. In November 2017, he quit and joined a cousin working at a nearby baked goods factory but has since returned to working at a local poultry processing facility.

Like so many Karen in Sandville and Pineville, Hser Gay had no compunction about quitting a job. In some cases, with the right planning, someone can finish a job on Friday and start a new job on Monday at one of the other poultry plants or in different industries. The Karen are no longer dependent on the poultry plants as more companies in the region hire more Karen men and women.

When I met Hser Gay in December 2017 at a birthday party for Sam Ber's son, I was concerned with his overall health. He had gained a lot of weight, seemed withdrawn and directionless, and received another DUI (driving under the influence) while living with his parents in Sandville. He had never liked rural living, and I felt that he longed for the bright lights of Des Moines. But he stayed.

In July 2019, somewhat surprisingly, Hser Gay married a Sgaw Karen girl from Pineville. They lived with her parents until 2021, when they, too, made the trek north back to Des Moines. They had their first child in late 2021.

Hser Ku Htoo, aka Gola

Unfortunately, Hser Ku Htoo (Sweet Cool Gold) did not write an essay on our first meeting, and neither of us can recall why. Fortunately, he offers some autobiographical account in the following letter he wrote to Secretary of State Hillary Clinton upon her visit to Burma in 2011.

> I am Karen were I from, Burma. Now I live in Georgia. I liked telling you, it's in the condition in Burma and my researches in USA about Karen. We are Karen people who like to live in peacefully and Freedly in our Karen State. The SPDC [State Peace and Development Council] took over our state and make a flee to other country. The Burmese soldiers came to the Karen village. They force men to be as a slave. My dad got forced to be slave one time. He got to carry heavy stuff he got kicked to the soldiers. People in village have to live with fearness and there is no protection. They have to play it on to survive. If they heard the Burmese soldier arrived in the village, all people run to the juggle and hide. Because of this condition my family couldn't live in Burma and we flee to Thailand. We shelter in the refugee camp, live in the camp as a safe place but sometime with your. Living in the camp for me is just like living in jail. We can't go outside the camp and there is no way to make money and lower education and less aid.
>
> I am so excited to hear that you're going see the Burmese government. In this case I would like you to ask him to give back Karen State, no more killing people, no more burning the village include; who, crop and farm. I have a suggestion which is to give back our Karen State, free all ethnic group in Burma, no more worse the people as a slave and to make Burma become democracy country I hope that you can carry this objection to the Burmese government and help real people in Burma.[10]

Hser Ku Htoo, aka Gola (his nickname stems from his darker complexion; Gola Thu is the Karen word for Black Muslims as far as I can surmise), was born in Mae La Refugee Camp in 1995. He was twelve years old upon resettlement to the United States and fifteen years old when we met in 2010. He attended school in Mae La Camp until the fourth grade. He can read, speak, and write in Sgaw Karen, although with less proficiency than his older siblings. He spoke and wrote English with major grammar and pronunciation errors when we first met and has always demonstrated excellent listening skills. My first account of Hse Ku reads as follows:

> Comments: Hser Ku demonstrates an unwillingness to speak English. He demonstrates major pronunciation issues. I could not understand most of his speech. He tends to mumble and does not speak above an incoherent whisper. He also seems reticent and uninterested in studying. He seemed least interested in my arrival as a tutor! Like Hser Gay, he is very shy.[11]

Hser Ku was the only child placed in a sheltered ESOL (English to Speakers of Other Languages) class upon arrival in Arizona. He remained in a sheltered ESOL class for one semester. He was placed in the eighth

Figure 5.4. Hser Ku Htoo (2011). © Daniel Gilhooly

grade for one semester in Phoenix before relocating to Sandville. Upon arrival in Georgia, he was placed in eighth grade again. Hser Ku never attended the fifth, sixth, or seventh grades. Like many students who receive English support, he was placed by age rather than his language and academic abilities. He finished his junior year at Sandville High School with an overall GPA of 84 percent and 100 percent attendance. He graduated from high school in Des Moines in 2013.

His 2011 WIDA scores were most aligned with my own assessment of his English language proficiency. He had an overall score of 363 out of 600 (3.0 proficiency level out of 6), which places him on the lower level of the developing level. The only score that was of some surprise was his speaking score of 358 out of 600 (3.4 proficiency level out of 6) or developing. His highest score was in writing with a 387 out of 600 (3.5 proficiency level out of 6), which delighted me as we worked a lot on his writing.

As the youngest of the three adolescent brothers, Gola was nearly silent for the first months we worked together. Within our little group, he chose to defer to his brothers on most topics and points of discussion. In time, I would learn that Gola was the family comedian and could lighten the mood.

As a 1.5 generationer (he resettled at age twelve), Gola was less embedded in Karen culture and showed less awareness of Sgaw Karen history, culture, language, the insurgency, or Karen nationalism. While his brothers or father related stories about Burma or Karen mythology, he remained silent but attentive. I believe he learned much about Karen culture via our collaborative research.

Gola enjoys cooking, fashion, soccer, gaming, and Facebook. Although he lacks the natural athleticism of his brothers, he sometimes played soccer and cane ball with a tenacity that belied his usual lackadaisical attitude. Other days he stayed home and did not join in whatever game we were playing that day.

Hser Ku has an uncanny sense of fashion and made the most of his donated wardrobe. I was amazed how well he could put together outfits in the latest pan-Asian styles he emulated from Korean K-pop, Thai, and even Karen stars.

He was often the butt of jokes from his father and brothers and ridiculed for his lack of athletic prowess. He fought hard in our matches but could not match the ability and dexterity of his brothers on the cane ball court. Despite his silence and occasional one-liners, he proved to be a very considerate young man who was always attentive to my needs and preferences. He served me drinks and lunch without prompting at every visit in those early days. He silently served me bottles of water rather than Mellow Yellow when he noticed cans set before me went untouched. When our lessons concluded, Gola would invariably and silently pack my bags, organize the video gear, and lug everything out to my car.

Of all the brothers, I developed the closest relationship with Gola. We chat from time to time on Messenger, and we always spend time together when I visit. I am always impressed with his intelligence, consideration, commitment to his parents, and sense of humor. We often have deep discussions about girls, school, religion, parents, and the challenges of life. He is a young man caught between two cultures but demonstrates a maturity that encourages me that he is up for the challenge. Out of all the brothers, he is the only one to embrace American food, television, and popular culture. We now share dinners and a beer when I visit. He has become like a younger brother for whom I have always felt a special fondness.

Des Moines

When the family relocated to Des Moines in 2012, Gola went into his senior year of high school. He never complained and seemed indifferent to the idea of restarting once again in a new place and a new school. He graduated from Hoover High School in Des Moines in 2013. He then attended community college for one semester. For financial reasons, he quit school and began working with Sam Ber at the packaging company. We always spent time together during my biannual visits to Iowa, and I was concerned with his lack of socialization. According to his own admission, he worked part-time and slept most of the day when he was not working.

He joined the family when they returned to Georgia in 2014 and became the sole breadwinner, supporting his parents and younger brother. As the oldest child living with his parents, Gola took on all the responsibilities once held by his older brothers. After only two years working at the poultry plant, he saved nearly $30,000 to help purchase the family home. His weekly income at the time was $340.

Upon our last meeting in December 2019, I was impressed with Hser Ku's achievements and overall attitude. He is still an affable young guy who works hard and socializes with Karen friends on the weekends. He expressed an interest in returning to community college or investing in a small business with Karen friends. He seems to have learned from the trials of his brothers and found some happiness. Yet, I think he feels a yearning for something more. We have talked about collaborating again as researchers, and this seemed to offer a spark of hope. For now, he is trying to make as much money as he can and enjoy his free time with his Karen buddies.

Ler Moo

Unlike his brothers, Ler Moo is considered a 1.75 generationer. He shares characteristics of second-generation immigrants who are less aware of Karen culture and language. At age seven, he arrived in the United States and has very little experience or memory of Burma or the camps.

I met Ler Moo when he was nine years old. Ler Moo was the shyest, but we became buddies over the ensuing months, and he opened up to me. We often laughed and joked, but his English was often unintelligible, and I often found myself just going along with him with a smile. After the first few months, it was clear that Ler Moo was not a talker in English or Karen, and now after ten years, he is even less vocal.

Ler Moo was typical in many ways of a 1.75 generationer and had many advantages not afforded his brothers. The most important was his friendship with Michael, a classmate and someone who lived within a long walk or biking distance from the Htoo home. Michael's family had taken Ler Moo under their wing, and most days, he was at their home, or Michael was hanging out with us at the Htoo home.

Ler Moo was unassuming and silent in each setting, at Michael's house, playing or studying at home, or on the ball field. As his language tutor, his silence was frustrating. I grew concerned with Ler Moo not long before his family moved to Des Moines. I was concerned that despite socialization,

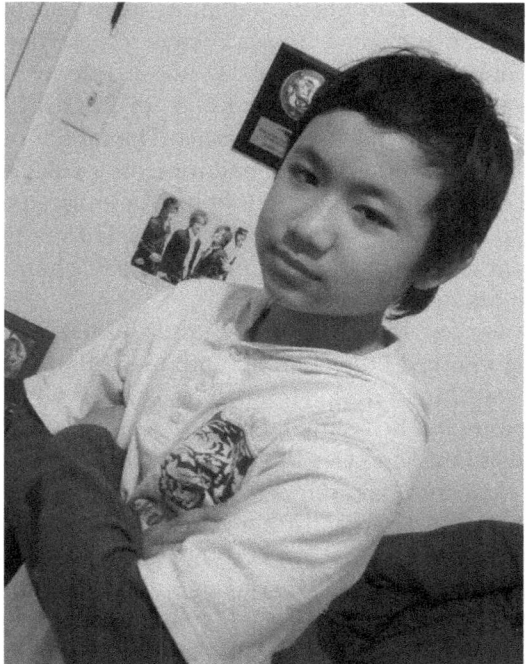

Figure 5.5. Ler Moo (2012). © Daniel Gilhooly

schooling, and my tutoring, his language was not improving. He simply would not speak unless directly asked a question.

He was a reluctant speaker, but the muffled whispers were only one concern as his spoken language was almost indiscernible. His grades were always very good, and he was in many ways a model student who was always polite and respectful. I encouraged him to take Michael's parents' offer to sign him up for soccer and baseball, and to my surprise, he asked them to register him for baseball and soccer. I was excited to observe him within a bigger, different social group. I was sure that his successes on the field would provide him the confidence he needed to begin to speak in English.

One of my most distinct impressions of Ler Moo was his uncanny ability as an athlete. He was a prodigy in every sport I saw him play. Soon after learning baseball and long before he had any idea of all the rules, he was the best player on his town team. He could hit, pitch, and play the field with equal acumen. He was even more talented at soccer and played on a town team. I encouraged him to continue to pursue baseball, but he only shrugged and gave me the Ler Moo smile, which to this day, I am afraid to admit, I am unable to read.

While he was accepted and included in the team and admired for his skill, he stayed much the same. I was always struck that despite more social involvement through sports, there was no discernible change in his attitude toward speaking in either Karen or English. I began to ask his brothers about his Karen language ability. The family primarily spoke Karen at home, and I wondered if he had more of a voice in Karen. They also expressed concern and indicated that his Karen language skills were limited, and he spoke sparingly within the family. His grades were always good, and I was always surprised that none of the teachers reached out to the family about his silence in school.

My concerns for Ler Moo heightened after he left Sandville for Des Moines. While he showed little emotion with the departure, I feel that the loss of Michael was devastating. He uttered very few words on the drive north to Des Moines, but he seemed his usual self when we hung out after arriving. Each visit I made to Des Moines from 2012 to 2014 increased my concern. It was clear that he rarely left the house except to attend school. He was gaining weight at an alarming rate as well. He gave up playing sports at school and seemed to want nothing more than to stay inside and play video games with his six-year-old nephew or shoot pool with his brothers in the basement. On each visit, I would take him and Hser Ku out to some activity like a movie or mini-golf, and he was unchanged, silent, and only minimally responsive. It was clear that there were no cognitive or developmental issues, but his family and I were concerned.

When the family moved back to Georgia in 2014, I initially saw Ler Moo a few times, but he seemed indifferent to my visits and even more isolated. I had finished my PhD and was working three teaching jobs, and had less time to visit. He was in high school when they returned, but as their new home was on the other side of the county, he was placed in a different high school from his former friends, Michael in particular. I found it strange, as did Michael, that Ler Moo made no attempts to meet or contact him. Ler Moo seemed content to help his parents around the house, watch videos, and play games on his phone. His sedate lifestyle added weight gain, and overall he did not look healthy. Sam Ber called me aside on one visit and indicated that the family was concerned with his silence and lack of will to leave the house. When I asked other Karen kids about him, they all said they never saw him at church or any other Karen gatherings.

Today, when I visit on my biannual trips, I am lucky to see Ler Moo as he will often stay in his room, and on my last visit, for the first time he did not "come out" to see me. I was shocked, hurt, and concerned. Sadly, these visits only last a few days, and there is no time to catch up and see if he might reveal something that I have missed all along.

What concerns me most about Ler Moo is that he has no foundation in any language or culture. He is truly caught between two cultures and languages without a steady footing in either. Whereas his brothers live mostly within their respective Karen communities, Ler Moo seems to belong in neither. His English is still difficult to understand, and his Karen is still limited, so I am unsure that he has a complete grasp of either. His willingness to communicate has remained tepid, and his unwillingness to socialize continues to worry me. Is he a by-product of so much uprooting? He lived in the camps, a year with his mother in Burma along the border (it has never been clear to me why they lived together outside the camps, but I was told that Esther was a teacher), moved to Phoenix, then Sandville, Des Moines, and back to Sandville. My own life has been peripatetic since the age of thirteen, and I empathize with Ler Moo, as I often have felt rootless. I know how hard it can be to uproot and start anew and wonder if Ler Moo decided that it was too tough to keep adjusting and has made the fateful decision to protect himself, internalize, and stay silent.

After graduating high school in 2016, Ler Moo began work at the poultry processing plant with other Karen but is the only brother working at his particular facility. He spends all his free time at home and helps his parents tend the chickens and work their ever-growing garden. Ler Moo seems to be a unique case as I am unfamiliar with similar instances of someone not proficient in any language. He continues to say very little at home, and the family seems somewhat resigned to his silence, but I have heard his brothers continue to express concern. I feel that I have failed him and that at some point, my own life became so hectic with marriage and the quick succession of two children that our bond eroded, and when I should have tried harder to reach him, I, too, resigned myself to his sheltered life. He is an enigma to me still today, and the writing of his story has helped me recognize how I have failed him as his teacher and older brother.

Notes

According to *Karen Proverbs*, this Karen proverb means, "Some are more fortunate than others." Drum Publications, *Karen Proverbs*, 22.

1. Rumbaut, "Ages, Life Stages, and Generational Cohorts," 1167.
2. Rumbaut, "Ages, Life Stages, and Generational Cohorts," 1167.
3. Rumbaut, "Ages, Life Stages, and Generational Cohorts," 1167.
4. Rumbaut, "Ties that Bind."
5. Rumbaut and Ima, *Adaptation of Southeast Asian Refugee Youth*, 22.

6. Field notes, 1 May 2010.
7. Personal communication, September 2013.
8. Field notes, 1 May 2010.
9. Unofficial transcript, Spring 2012.
10. Letter to Secretary of State Hillary Clinton from Hser Ku Htoo, 27 November 2011.
11. Field notes, 1 May 2010.

Conclusion

Implications and Limitations

The Salween River will never run dry;
a buffalo's horn will never be straight.

—Karen proverb

While recently discussing this book with a colleague, I was asked a question I have often considered over the past eleven years, "Are the Htoos happy?" My colleague asked this question so matter-of-factly that it seemed to suggest that it was the only question that mattered. The question also seemed to suggest that the answer would reveal some fundamental truth about the efficacy of the resettlement of families like the Htoos. After a long pause, all I could muster was a halfhearted, "I don't know." The colleague was dissatisfied, and the conversation soon ended. I continue to ask myself the same question with no more of an answer. It all seems far more complicated than a question of happiness.

Life in the United States has provided the family with much of what they hoped for when they decided to resettle. They have safety and security, employment, food, the freedom to express themselves without fear of persecution, and education for their children. They are afforded comforts they could never have imagined back in the camps like TVs, computers, refrigerators, and an endless supply of water, food, plumbing, electricity, and Wi-Fi.

For the children, they reside in the blurry borderlands between two cultures. Some with more of a foothold in American culture but, so far, the Htoos, like other Karen I have worked with, are firmly ensconced in one of the many Karen bubbles formed throughout the Karen diaspora.

Acculturation?

Brown and Esther live in retirement much as they would have back in Burma. Both garden, read the Bible, attend church services, and dote on their grandkids when they visit. They speak daily with friends and family across the globe via new technologies. They live almost exclusively within the margins of American society and are content. Neither their children nor grandchildren have acculturated in many ways, but each has been affected by the acculturation of friends, relatives, and loved ones.

Pamela Balls Organista, Gerardo Marín, and Kevin M. Chun define acculturation as "a culture learning process experienced by individuals who are exposed to a new culture or ethnic."[1] As such, after fifteen years in the country, there is little evidence that anyone in the family has acculturated namely because there is so little interaction with "American" culture. Each of the children drives cars and not motorbikes as they would in Thailand or Burma and, I am sure, their jobs look much different than what "work" would look like in Burma or the camps but their lives in many ways are much like how life would be in Burma, at least for those in Sandville. Communities like Sandville are particularly "better off" as their rural setting has softened the culture shock associated with resettlement.[2] But it has kept them isolated and, most likely, added to their lack of acculturation.

While all of the Htoo family members stay within their Karen enclaves, prefer to speak Sgaw Karen, and have limited interactions with other Americans, there are signs of alternative forms of acculturation. It is clear that all the Htoos, even Brown and Esther, are engaged in various forms of digital acculturation.[3] Each of the brothers is "on Facebook" regularly, and although these interactions are predominately with other ethnic Karen, they do maintain ties with "American friends" from various experiences in school, church, and work. The brothers also create and disseminate music, videos, and other content, and some are regular gamers and "belong" to the gaming community. These Web 2.0 spaces serve as important means of retaining connections with those outside their ethnic enclave. It seems that even though the Htoos each maintain at least some traditional Karen beliefs and values, other Karen are acculturating as they appropriate more Western ideas and values. This has been most evident among Karen girls and women.

The marital issues that both the elder Htoo brothers experienced seem to stem from their wives' preference for American attitudes toward dating, marriage, and women's rights. I was told many times by the brothers that Karen "don't date." Based on my observations, this seems very much true for many. Rather than dating, couples either marry straight away or are engaged for years before marrying. Some of these "engagements" lead to marriage, and others do not. I have heard multiple accounts of Karen women bucking this tradition and dating outside the Karen community, having children without marrying, or leaving their Karen spouses to marry outside the Karen community. Though the brothers expected more traditional Karen relationships, it seems that their spouses have been influenced by more modern American perceptions about dating and marriage that have impacted the course of their and their children's lives.

For parents like Brown and Esther, who feel it is too late for them in the United States—too late to learn the language, too late to acculturate, too late to feel at home—I wonder if there is not a sense of disappointment or a feeling that expectations have gone unrealized. They have never expressed as much to me or through their children, but I feel this is due more to politeness or fear of seeming ungrateful. The children are more forthcoming. And there are signs of a change of heart on many fronts.

After fifteen years in the United States, there is no longer any talk of returning home. Home is now Sandville and Des Moines. None of the Htoos speak of returning to the camps or Burma as they once did. Esther returned in the fall of 2019 to visit family still in the camps, and that was enough. Things have changed, and Mae La Camp is now providing shelter for the latest generation fleeing persecution and it, too, has changed. For the children, there are no longer grand ambitions of becoming doctors that return to serve in the camps or great ideas of returning to join the fight. Rather, today they speak of the present and surviving.

I recently received a message from Hser Gay Htoo that read: "Any ideas on a side hustle to make some extra money?" After I got over the unexpected idiomatic usage of "side hustle," I tried to think of ways they could make a quick buck but responded with "buy and then sell a used car?" Like many other Karen, I noticed that the Htoos would buy cheap used cars and discard them once they no longer functioned. I always thought the brothers could make a small business of finding reliable vehicles to sell at a small profit within the Karen community. His only response was, "I have no cars." But his question was telling. He works long hours and just had his first child and needs a hustle to survive.

Some of their goals have been achieved, but none of the expected dividends. While all four brothers earned a high school diploma, none could leverage their diploma to escape the poultry plants or other low-skilled jobs in factories. And though they have worked hard, saved their money, and, for the most part, played by the rules, they must defer to future generations to attain the dreams they once held among the early optimism of coming to the United States. While the brothers find their jobs tolerable or what they call "easy," there has been an increasing sense within our recent conversations that they want more and are coming to the realization that their futures are less full of promise. Failed marriages and dead-end jobs are not unique to resettled refugees, but dreams deferred seem a rite of passage for resettled refugees like the Htoos in the United States.

And what frustrates me and makes me wonder whether this book offers anything new to the debates about refugee resettlement is how little has changed. This account of the Htoos mirrors earlier accounts of Hmong, Vietnamese, Cambodian, and the myriad others who have come to the United States since the Refugee Act of 1980.

When I think of the brothers' American experience, I realize that most of their interactions outside their Karen community were/are with me, at school, at work, or through the American Baptist youth group. Otherwise, occasional trips to Walmart or the nearby grocery and the doctor's office continue to be their only "American" experiences. And these outings are rare as most of their food is grown or bought from other Karen (vegetables and meat) or at the Asian grocery in Atlanta. Restaurants, sporting events, fast food, the bank, the post office, the hairdresser, movie theaters, amusement parks, the mechanic, bowling alleys, and other typical American institutions are as foreign to them as when they first arrived.

I always have the sense that the brothers and most of the Karen children and adults I know best are still somewhat uncomfortable outside their Karen community—not all but most. The brothers often lamented the lack of social opportunities living in rural isolation but what they missed were interactions with Karen of their age. In some ways, language and culture shock is still a part of their American experience after fifteen years in the country. This may lend credence to the argument that ethnic enclaves do not lend themselves to acculturation. Today, when I visit them in Sandville, I realize how reluctant some are to venture out.

Maybe it is as simple as economics and time. As their salaries increase, so will their active participation in American life. Because of its ruralness, I have often wondered if some Karen might not break away and live, like the Amish, within but apart. It is doubtful but, like the Amish, they have a version of Christianity better suited to the seventeenth century. I know that creating their own religio-cultural community, isolated amongst the pine forests of eastern Georgia, was a plan of sorts at one point as more Karen families moved to the area. Today, the Karen community in Sandville is in flux.

While the Htoos may not represent acculturation, the signs are loud and clear. The first Karen cheerleader graduated from Sandville High School in 2020. And the first Karen to graduate from a four-year institution will graduate from the University of Georgia in the spring of 2022! Others are marrying outside the Karen community. But the price is much the same for those like the Htoo family, who are the first to come.

Happiness may be a privilege stalled for resettlers like the Htoos as they cope with the daily responsibilities of life in their new land.

Implications for Teaching and Learning

For decades, we have known that the experiences of older resettled adolescents like Moe Tha Wah are often marked by isolation, a lack of English language proficiency, and limited educational opportunities that lead to limited professional opportunities. Yet, very little seems to have changed in addressing the unique needs of these 1.25 generationers. These individuals need extra support, and more efforts are needed to help these youth integrate into the school and broader community. As a society, we need to question the assumption that all immigrants must suffer like previous generations to earn a livable income and have equitable educational opportunities.

And the answers have long been known. Each of the brothers would have benefited from more participation in extracurricular activities. Karen parents need to know that participation in such programs is beneficial. And, as the brothers, researchers, teachers, and teacher-educators have long known, everything is rooted in English language development. As a nation, we spend little on our refugee resettlement program, and more needs to be allocated for programs that can make a difference. It seems that the new world order will include ever-increasing numbers of refugees, so there is no end in sight to the needs of families like the Htoos to find a place to begin anew.

For schools like Sandville, overwhelmed by the arrival of Karen students, something needs to be done in advance. Teachers and staff need to be aware of who the students are, where they are from, and what language(s) they speak. Teachers have to have training on the various ways they can promote inclusion in classrooms. Teachers need to know that they are English language teachers even if it is not spelled out in their contracts. Schools need to provide training to all staff in terms of their role in making all social spaces of the schoolyard, the hallway, the bus, and the cafeteria places for language development. Efforts to create a culture of inclusion in schools need to be made for culturally and linguistically diverse (CLD) students like the Karen. This includes information sessions for teachers, staff, and the student bodies.

The brothers were eager to tell their stories, but no opportunities were provided to talk about their life experiences and cultural background with classmates or staff. While some teachers encouraged them to share information about their culture, few teachers even knew anything about them.

This is a lost opportunity for the students, their school peers, and the local community.

Our research collaboration gleaned important data on Karen resettlement experiences and provided the brothers a learning opportunity that showcased their knowledge and skills. By interviewing other Karen in their language, they found value in their home language. Students' home language(s) continue to be a lost resource in classrooms, and too many teachers, parents, and students feel they must shed their home language on the way to learning English. Teachers need training on ways home languages can be integrated into teaching without jeopardizing curricular goals. And, at the very least, schools need to make it clear to parents that the home language is an important part of their child's cognitive, emotional, psychological, and overall language development and that parents play a role in promoting all domains of language at home.

More language support is also needed for these students. The brothers each complained about the lack of explicit language instruction they received in their schools. As Sam Ber lamented: "How can I learn economics when I don't know English? We need English first." Teaching English often falls on unprepared teachers to meet their students' unique language and academic needs. And even when teachers are trained, it is not easy to teach heterogeneous classes of students with varying proficiencies in their home language and English. More one-on-one tutoring needs to be made available as it can lead to positive outcomes, as discussed in this book.

Teacher training in higher education must include some commitment to helping all pre-service teachers understand and strategize on ways to best serve students like the Htoos. For the past six years, I have taught multiple graduate level cohorts of in-service teachers who work at high population CLD schools. The vast majority of my students are elementary school teachers, and I have yet to have any teacher from high school, where, it could be argued, the greatest needs exist. The Htoo brothers exemplify this need.

At a time in American history when issues around immigration and questions abound and are polarized, resettler youth can serve as important voices and examples of both the hardships of resettlement and the successes when schools are prepared to meet their needs. Diverse students bring rich knowledge and experiences to their schools and communities. Children like the Htoos have demonstrated great resilience and commitment to school, that should be a model for all students. Despite their expressed disillusionment with the system, all of the brothers maintained 100 percent attendance records and continue to support themselves and their families through hard work in jobs they tolerate.

Much has been written regarding the need to recognize and incorporate students' funds of knowledge into classroom instruction, yet this is often not evidenced in schools and less often in communities. I have found no lack of interested volunteers who are willing to help families like the Htoos, but they are often not utilized and are unprepared. Classmates of students like the Htoos are also missing out on expanding their worldviews on issues like immigration, war, trauma, and the realities associated with adapting to a new culture and language. The Sandville schools have had Karen students for more than ten years, but there is still little acknowledgment of their background.

The Htoo brothers have been fortunate in some respects. They were able to access support in the form of an in-home tutor like me and leveraged the willingness of neighbors to assist them in all and sundry. This should be one of the options schools have when allocating resources. Trained peer tutors can fill an important gap in language education. Moreover, less formal language socialization programs can be established. Native English-speaking peers can earn service credit or other recognition for serving as peer language tutors. These peer tutors can provide important social interactional ties as well as meaningful English language opportunities as well.

Programs that incorporate other community institutions can be effective and meaningful to all participants. Establishing language partnerships with willing members of local community centers or retirement complexes can offer important socialization opportunities for both local seniors and culturally diverse students and families.

Academics, teachers, and policymakers have recognized the importance of parent-school relations for many decades yet the Htoo parents never attended a parent-teacher conference. After nearly ten years of having children in the American education system, few of the Karen families in Sandville attend a parent-teacher night. The Htoo parents had high regard for their child's education but that high regard was very much ambivalent. Moreover, they discounted that they could be of any value in their child's education when they had such limited formal education and felt inadequate in their English language ability.

Parents need to be encouraged to help support their child's learning and socialization and educated about issues surrounding grading, report cards, homework, and the benefits of extracurricular activities for their children. For Esther and Brown Htoo, playing sports or participating in the band were not considered important aspects of their child's education. Parents need to see the value in such activities for their child's overall social-emotional, cognitive, linguistic, and physical development.

Parents also need to know the important role they play in helping their children develop their home language skills. If CLD parents are literate in the home language, resources can be found so that parents can read to their children. For the Sgaw Karen, online publications like Drum Publications offer free and paid resources that teachers and parents can use. Moreover, teachers need to be listened to and supported.

For older 1.25 generation students like Moo Tha Wah, schools must employ pragmatic approaches. Every effort must be made first to address the need for oral competence in English. Too many schools cannot play catch up with students like Moo Tha Wah. His is a cautionary tale of how a lack of English language ability and overall understanding of how various systems work can lead to unfortunate outcomes.

He and his spouse would have also benefited from understanding what it means to be a parent in the United States. Parental roles differ across cultures. Parenting and marriage are not easy under "normal" circumstances, and I cannot imagine how complicated expectations of self and partner must be for young couples like Sam Ber and Moe Tha Wah and their spouses. In the United States, divorce comes with monetary and legal obligations that differ from how things would be handled in Burma or the camps.

Schools, churches, community centers, and other organizations currently offering language courses must begin providing training on those functional literacies needed to navigate everyday life in the United States. These functional literacies include learning how to: fill out applications, buy a car, access services like Supplemental Nutrition Assistance Program (SNAP) or locate local English language courses, apply for citizenship, vote, access an attorney, pay bail, interact with police or medical professionals in times of crisis, navigate the medical system, access insurance for health, home, and automobile. They also need to be taught about various processes and procedures related to buying a home, paying taxes, finding legal support, and a host of other procedures that mark the American experience. Too many children are burdened with these parental responsibilities, and too many parents are taking a back seat to their children who tend to take on parental responsibilities because of their relative proficiency in English.

The Karen in the United States are relatively lucky as they have such a well-established network through various churches yet they, too, need support through educational programs. Churches of all denominations have recruited Karen into their churches, but they seem to have an agenda. Recently, multiple churches have been vying for Karen membership, which has caused rifts. The Karen are proving to be very amenable to the church that offers the most material support.

Post-Secondary Education

More post-secondary education options need to be available for students like the Htoo brothers. I have observed a troubling trend related to community and technical college programs like the one Hser Ku Htoo attended for one semester. These schools require that students take English language courses before or while pursuing other programs. Multiple Karen graduates from Sandville and neighboring Pineville started at a local technology school but eventually dropped out. I remember the frustration of one Karen student who showed me his reading for his English course. It was an article discussing gender identity from a post-modern perspective. He had underlined nearly every sentence in the first few paragraphs of the reading, telling me he had no idea what the article was about. Some language is required to become a plumber or auto mechanic, but insights into post-modern perceptions of gender seem better left elsewhere. By accessing post-secondary programs, Karen and other immigrants and refugees have more skills to offer their communities. Reassessing how these technical and community college programs are structured is a first step in making programs more available post-high school.

Church and State

Chapter 1 revealed the effect American Christian missionaries had on the Sgaw Karen people, and this relationship continues in communities like Sandville and across the Karen diaspora. Some churches promote political agendas that do not always serve immigrants or refugee interests. Surprisingly, most older Karen I talked to speak about how Karen churches fully supported President Trump despite anti-immigrant and anti-refugee policies.

Under the Trump administration, the US government all but shut down the refugee resettlement program and thus cut funding to the voluntary organizations (VOLAGS) who do the heavy lifting in the US refugee resettlement program. This means caseworkers were no longer available, language classes were shut down, and important support staff lost jobs. Moreover, policies on filing for citizenship have changed, adding new financial burdens on already cash-strapped refugee families. Waivers on fees for processing have been eliminated. This means that those individuals over the age of eighteen who want to become citizens must pay a couple of thousand dollars to be processed. Most had qualified for a waiver because of their low incomes. The Trump era also altered public opinion toward immigrants and refugees. Refugees were deported, including some Karen, who were deported to Burma, a country they may have never lived in before.[4] Refugees have become politicized.

Before the 2020 presidential election, President Trump warned at a rally in Minnesota: "Biden will turn Minnesota into a refugee camp, and he said that. Overcrowding public resources, overcrowding schools, and inundating your hospitals. You know that. It's already there, it's a disgrace. What they have done to your state, it's absolutely a disgrace."[5]

This us-against-them mentality makes life for resettlers uncomfortable at best, and, at worst, they become targets of violent xenophobia. Yet, many Karen pastors were actively encouraging their Karen congregants to vote for Trump in 2020. Many of those who help the Karen in Sandville and around the country are often vocal Trump supporters, yet they seem to live in the space of cognitive dissonance. I remember one of the Htoos most valued "American" (white) friends and neighbors, Mr. Matt (pseudonym), railing against "foreigners" coming to this country "to live off our social services and have babies." Yet, he welcomed his Karen neighbors and has been a great help to many. I still do not understand it, but I have seen the possible harm such strange bedfellows make.

The senior pastor of Sandville Baptist Karen Church, his wife, and his daughter died of COVID-19, and many others have been sick from the virus. This is largely due to the false narratives disseminated across Karen "media" platforms from around the world about the dangers of vaccines. Refugees are vulnerable to political and other types of manipulation. As one Karen told me, "Karen will believe anything if a white pastor says it."[6]

In addition to political awareness, refugee-background families need to know their legal rights as permanent residents and citizens. The Htoos would have benefited from more formal training on these kinds of topics either before arrival or soon after resettlement. If it were not for local supporters like Ms. Julia (pseudonym) from Jubilee Partners and, to a lesser extent, me, families rely on dubious reports from fellow Karen and neighbors like Mr. Matt.

Training Pre-Arrival

The Htoo story also demonstrates the importance of training before resettlement. Systems must be put in place to prepare families for the education, legal, housing, health care, and other realities of the American experience. English language classes should also be made available well in advance of resettlement. Refugee life in the camps is often marked by boredom and a lack of purpose, but this time can be better leveraged. Three-day cultural seminars as those offered to the Htoos before their departure to the United States are inadequate. Programs can and should be established with universities or other organizations to train teachers to work within the refugee camps as part of their education programs. Karen youth must also be recognized as a part of the solution.

Many young Karen who are active in local, regional, and national Christian youth organizations are gaining important skills that teachers and schools need to recognize, promote, and utilize. These funds of knowledge of Karen youth are wide and diverse. The Htoo children all have years of experience with animal husbandry, planting and maintaining gardens, memorization of religious texts and Karen parables, and digital media from recording music to creating videos shared on sites like You-Tube. Karen youth also demonstrate a proclivity toward music, sports, and drawing, which can be capitalized upon in their schooling.

Karen youth should be utilized in collaborative research efforts as the one described earlier. Their involvement can help shape future leaders within the community. Such research projects teach real data collection and organization skills and how information can be disseminated. Ideally, many of these youth will return to lead or in other capacities to support those still in the refugee camps.

Policy Implications

The collective story of the Htoo family and their individual experiences offer considerations for policymakers. The US refugee resettlement program is undergoing a major revaluation after the Trump administration, the COVID-19 pandemic, and the new Biden administration. While I in no way condone the gutting of the refugee resettlement program, it may provide a unique starting point for future administrations designing a new resettlement program. As noted earlier, more needs to be done by the various governmental and non-governmental agencies related to pre-resettlement training. Investments pre-resettlement for language classes, US civics, and other important information can have long-term cost benefits and will make for easier adjustment. Those refugees who are confined to camps and looking to resettle have the time and motivation to learn as much as they can about Western education, laws, and lifestyles.

A minimum of one year of English courses should be mandatory for all newly resettled adolescents over the age of seventeen and adults. These classes should combine both language training and information about the legal rights, laws, and classes related to Western parenting and the role parents play in American schools. These courses could also provide language training specific to the various industries that most often employ refugees. Once these language and culture courses end, participants should have assistance in seeking employment.

Secondary Migration

The Htoo family demonstrates how transient resettlers are as they relocate for better jobs, family reunification, or other reasons. Under the current system, once a family moves from their initial resettlement town or city, they lose access to valuable caseworkers. There must be more flexibility when providing support after moving from their initial resettlement.

Leaders within the community should be identified and then utilized. These leaders can help disseminate information via digital technologies. Karen networks should be acknowledged and used as another means of sharing information and addressing misinformation.

The United States needs to reconsider the current policy regarding resettlers repaying airfare costs. This practice only burdens already cash-strapped families and hinders economic self-sufficiency. The amount of financial assistance for newly resettled families needs to be reevaluated. The Htoo family received approximately $1,000 upon arrival and three months of paid rent. This is not enough for a family of seven. Economic independence can be better realized if more is invested pre- and post-arrival. Refugees continue to serve as a significant labor source in important economic sectors in agriculture, manufacturing, and meat processing. These jobs should be seen as providing first-generation adult refugees a means for initial employment and a stepping stone to other opportunities. As the COVID-19 pandemic has demonstrated, protections need to be put in place in these industries to protect the rights of workers who are often taken advantage of because of their lack of English and fear of dismissal.

Information services need to be provided to help families better navigate the legal system in the United States. Moo Tha Wah's story is not unique, and his fear of the unknown further complicates legal entanglements like his. More awareness initiatives need to be created about the risks of drugs and alcohol, an issue with the Htoo children and other Karen in the United States.

Transformations and Limitations

The past eleven years working with the Htoos and the wider Karen community in the United States have been transformative for me. My research has provided me with deep human connections that do not fall in any single relational category. The Htoos are friends, a surrogate family, and research collaborators/participants. I know that my time with these families, especially the Htoos, was marked by acceptance. In great part, they and all things Karen have become the primary focus of my time, reading, scholarship, and advocacy.

I transformed through the process and believe that the brothers were also changed by our time together. I am more empathetic, and I feel I am a better teacher. But the imbalance is clear. I continue, through my writing, to live in that time whereas the brothers have moved on and, though still close, I am no longer a daily part of any of their lives. Fortunately, some have found new advocates who have filled in the gaps. Ms. Julia now helps with paperwork, accessing services, and navigating US bureaucracy.

I have benefited professionally from my relationship with the Htoos and the wider Karen community. I have published articles, won awards, and traveled to present my research at conferences. I am currently tenured as an Associate Professor, and my career has advanced as a result of my work. This has always been in my mind from the earliest days. How can I write honestly about these people who have become in so many ways my closest companions without there being some exploitative element? I take some solace in the thought that our relationship was reciprocal. While their transformations may be less tangible, I think they each gained from our multidimensional relationship, and I am delighted when they reach out to me after years of separation. I see my work as longitudinal and my relationship with the Htoo family as a lifelong commitment.

The Brothers' Transformations

The brothers transformed in unexpected ways. As researchers, they learned through the process of creating and asking questions. They learned about their parents' lives in Burma before they were born, insight most of us only get glimpses of from old photographs and the memories of our parents.

I like to believe that they also gained a new understanding of what it means to be Karen as well as what it means to be an American. Our relationship also allowed them to consider their culture, history, language, and beliefs in ways that they may not have considered. It also led them to question or consider some of their family beliefs and consider new, more American ways of being.

Limitations

The biggest limitation that I bring to any book on the Sgaw Karen is my lack of Sgaw Karen language ability. While there were times during my research when the brothers or other members would teach me a few words or expressions, I was woefully negligent in my Karen language studies.

Speaking Karen would have allowed me more interactions with Brown, Esther, and the brothers. I will leave it to the individual reader to draw their conclusions on how great an impact this has had on the veracity of my understanding of Karen culture and the people who populate these pages. Our relationships were founded and developed via English, which implicitly provided me with a privileged position. I made efforts to compensate for this language divide by always demonstrating respect for and inclusion of Sgaw Karen in our collaborative research. Moreover, throughout this manuscript and other works on the Karen community in Sandville, I have tried to include Karen voices and opinions.

Although we did not share a common language and our life experiences were different, we shared some commonalities. Like the brothers, I relocated during early adolescence when my father accepted a job in Israel when I was thirteen years old. That transnational experiences gave me a unique connection with the brothers despite our differences. While my traumas pale in comparison to the deprivation the brothers faced in Thai refugee camps and resettlement in the United States, they have made me more aware of and empathetic to the brothers' experiences with language, socializing, and the trauma of separation from family and friends.

This book also fails to describe the experiences of female Karen in any depth. While Esther's story has some treatment, there is no female character within this narrative. I hope to rectify this in further publications.

Finally, I fear this book also contains information or characterizations that some readers may find offensive. For this, I apologize in advance. A reviewer very recently considered my use of "the Karen" as having an "exoticizing effect" and recommended I use "Karen people" instead. I have tried throughout to heed this advice. But I have been guilty of exoticizing in other ways that I must acknowledge.

Exoticizing

In my early days working with the Sgaw Karen community in Sandville, the Htoos and other Karen families were my primary topic of conversation with friends, classmates, and family. I soon found that though many were willing to listen, few shared my enthusiasm. I realized that most people were "interested" in the exotic, strange, and bizarre. So, in those early days, that is what I often shared with people. For this, I am regretful, as it does not meet with the ethics I have tried to maintain. What was bizarre, strange, and exotic was only a fragment of the picture of the people who inhabit these pages. I am unaware of similar misrepresentations and hope the reader would take the time to contact me and set me straight.

Notes

According to *Karen Proverbs*, this Karen proverb means, "Some things will never change." Drum Publications, *Karen Proverbs*, 9.

1. Organista et al., *Psychology of Ethnic Groups*, 102.
2. Gilhooly and Lee, "Rethinking Refugee Resettlement."
3. See Dey et al., "Digital Consumer Culture," 10.
4. Tun, "Myanmar Nationals Deported."
5. Chiu, "'Stunning in Ugliness and Tone.'"
6. Personal communication. February 15, 2021.

Bibliography

Barnett, Don. "A New Era of Refugee Resettlement." *Center for Immigration Studies*, 1 December 2006. Retrieved 15 May 2009 from https://cis.org/Report/New-Era-Refugee-Resettlement.

Barron, Sandy, John Okell, Saw Myat Yin, Kenneth VanBik, Arthur Swain, Emma Larkin, Anna J. Allott, and Kirsten Ewers. *Refugees from Burma: Their Backgrounds and Refugee Experience,* edited by Donald A. Ranard and Sandy Barron. Washington, DC: Center for Applied Linguistics, 2007. https://www.hplct.org/assets/uploads/files/refugeesfromburma.pdf.

Beech, Hannah. "We Were Bulletproof: As Child Soldiers Grow Up, Legacy of War Lingers." *New York Times,* 12 October 2020. Retrieved 2 March 2021 from https://www.nytimes.com/2020/10/12/world/asia/myanmar-thailand-gods-army-htoo-twins.html.

Boorman, John, dir. *Beyond Rangoon.* Culver City, CA: Columbia Pictures, 1995.

Bowles, Edith. "From Village to Camp: Refugee Camp Life in Transition on the Thailand-Burma border." *Forced Migration Review* 2 (1998): 11–14.

Brown, Rebekah. "'Our Words Are Very Little': The Untold Story of the Tasmanian Karen." PhD diss., University of Tasmania, 2018.

Buadaeng, Kwanchewan. *Ethnic Identities of the Karen Peoples in Burma and Thailand.* Berghahn Books: New York, 2007.

Cady, John. *A History of Modern Burma.* Ithaca, NY: Cornell University Press, 1958.

Case, Jay Riley. *An Unpredictable Gospel: American Evangelicals and World Christianity, 1812–1920.* New York: Oxford University Press, 2011.

Charney, Michael W. *A History of Modern Burma.* New York: Cambridge University Press, 2009.

Cheesman, Nick. "Seeing Karen in the Union of Myanmar." *Asian Ethnicity* 2 (2002): 199–220.

Chiu, Allyson. "'Stunning in Ugliness & Tone': Trump Denounced for Attacking Somali Refugees in Minnesota." *The Washington Post,* 11 October 2019. Retrieved 11 January 2021 from https://www.washingtonpost.com/nation/2019/10/11/trump-somali-refugees-minneapolis-rally/.

Cho, Violet. "Rearranging Beads on a Necklace: Reflections on Burmese Karen Media in Exile." *Inter-Asia Cultural Studies* 12, no. 3 (2011): 465–472.

——. "Searching for Home: Explorations in New Media and the Burmese Diaspora in New Zealand." *Pacific Journalism Review* 17, no. 1 (2011): 194–209.

Cusano, Chris. "Burma: Displaced Karens; Like Water on The Khu Leaf." In *Caught between Borders: Response Strategies of the Internally Displaced*, edited by Marc Vincent and Birgitte R. Sorenson, 138–171. London: Pluto Press, 2001.

Daewood, Noor. "From Persecution to Poverty: The Cost of the U.S. Refugee Program's Narrow Emphasis on Early Employment." *Berkeley Public Policy Journal*, 18 January 2011. Retrieved 2 January 2014 from https://bppj.berkeley .edu/2011/01/18/from-persecution-to-poverty-the-costs-of-the-u-s-refugee-resettlement-programs-narrow-emphasis-on-early-employment/.

de Jong, John. "A Nineteenth-Century New England Exegete Abroad: Adoniram Judson and the Burmese Bible." *Harvard Theological Review* 112, no. 3 (2019): 319–339.

Denzin, Norman K. *Interpretive Biography*, vol. 17. Newbury Park, CA: Sage, 1989.

Dey, Bidit L., Dorothy Yen, and Lalnunpuia Samuel. "Digital Consumer Culture and Digital Acculturation." *International Journal of Information Management* 51 (2020): 10–19.

Drum Publications Group. *Karen Proverbs*. Yumpu.com, August 2007. Retrieved 6 February 2011 from https://www.yumpu.com/en/document/read/2512220/karen-proverbs-drum-publications.

Dun, Smith. *Memoirs of the Four-Foot Colonel*. Ithaca, NY: Cornell University Press, 1980.

Falla, Jonathan. *True Love and Bartholomew: Rebels on the Burmese Border*. New York: Cambridge University Press, 1991.

Ferrars, Max, and Bertha Ferrars. *Burma*. New York: S. Low, Marston, Limited, 1900.

Forbes, Thomas R. "Midwifery and Witchcraft." *Journal of the History of Medicine and Allied Sciences* 2 (1962): 264–283.

Freire, Paulo. *Pedagogy of the Oppressed*. 50th Anniversary Edition. London: Bloomsbury Publishing, 2008.

Geertz, Clifford. *The Interpretation of Cultures*. New York: Basic Books, 1973.

Gilhooly, Daniel, Michelle Amos, and Christina Kitson. "Reading the Ink around Us: How Karen Refugee Youth Use Tattoos as an Alternative Literacy Practice." *Journal of Research in Childhood Education* 33, no. 1 (2019): 145–163.

Gilhooly, Daniel, Liaquat Channa, and Charles Allen Lynn. "Co-creating the Dialogic: How a Participatory Action Research Project Promoted Second Language Acquisition of Karen Youth." *Journal of Southeast Asian American Education and Advancement* 12, no. 1 (2017): Article 5.

Gilhooly, Daniel, and Eunbae Lee. "The Role of Digital Literacy Practices on Refugee Resettlement: The Case of Three Karen Brothers." *Journal of Adolescent & Adult Literacy* 57, no. 5 (2014): 387–396.

——. "Rethinking Urban Refugee Resettlement: A Case Study of One Karen Community in Rural Georgia, USA." *International Migration* 55, no. 6 (2017): 37–55.

Gilhooly, D., & Htoo, C. M. "More than Names on a Roster: The Many Meanings Behind Sgaw Karen Names." *Journal for Multicultural Education* 16, no. 2(2022): 195–206.

Glesne, C. *Becoming Qualitative Researchers: An Introduction*. Boston: Pearson 2011.

Gonzalez, Norma, Luis C. Moll, Martha Floyd-Tenery, Anna Rivera, Patricia Rendon, and Cathy Amanti. "Teacher Research on Funds of Knowledge: Learning from Households." UC Berkeley: Center for Research on Education, Diversity and Excellence. Retrieved 30 June 2022 from https://escholarship.org/uc/item/5tm6x7cm.

Gravers, Michael, ed. *Exploring Ethnic Diversity in Burma*. Copenhagen: NIAS Press, 2007.

Harriden, Jessica. "'Making a Name for Themselves': Karen Identity and the Politicization of Ethnicity in Burma." *Journal of Burma Studies* 7, no. 1 (2002): 84–144.

Hayami, Yoko. "Karen Tradition according to Christ or Buddha: The Implications of Multiple Reinterpretations for a Minority Ethnic Group in Thailand." *Journal of Southeast Asian Studies* 27, no. 2 (1996): 334–349.

Hayami, Yōko. *Between hills and plains: Power and practice in socio-religious dynamics among Karen*. Vol. 7. Trans Pacific Press, 2004.

Hein, Jeremy. "Refugees, Immigrants, and the State." *Annual Review of Sociology* 19, no. 1 (1993): 43–59.

Heppner, Kevin. *Sold to Be Soldiers: The Recruitment and Use of Child Soldiers in Burma*. Human Rights Watch, 31 October 2007. Retrieved 30 June 2022 from https://www.hrw.org/report/2007/10/31/sold-be-soldiers/recruitment-and-use-child-soldiers-burma.

Herrera, Socorro G. *Biography-Driven Culturally Responsive Teaching*. New York: Teachers College Press, 2016.

Jefferys, Kelly, and Daniel Martin. *Refugees and Asylees: 2017. Office of Immigration Statistics*, July 2008. Retrieved 2 February 2009 from https://www.dhs.gov/sites/default/files/publications/Refugees_Asylees_2007.pdf.

"Karen American Communities Foundation." *Karenamerican.org*. Retrieved 17 July 2010 from https://karenamerican.org/about-us/.

Karen American Communities Foundation (KACF). 2011. *Considerations for Individuals and Agencies Working with the Karen People of Burma in the United States*. Retrieved 1 September 2011 from http://karenusa.org/documents/Resources_for_Working_with_Karen_final_Nov.09.pdf. (No longer available online.)

Keyes, Charles F. *The Golden Peninsula: Culture and Adaptation in Mainland Southeast Asia*. Honolulu: University of Hawaii Press, 1994.

Krashen, Stephen D. "Bilingual Education and Second Language Acquisition Theory." In *Schooling and Language Minority Students: A Theoretical Framework*. 51–79. Los Angeles, CA: Evaluation, Dissemination and Assessment Center, 1981.

Kunz, Egon F. "The Refugee in Flight: Kinetic Models and Forms of Displacement." *International Migration Review* 7, no. 2 (1973): 125–146.

Lee, Sangkook. "The Adaptation and Identities of the Karen Refugees: A Case Study of Mae La Refugee Camp in Northern Thailand." Master's thesis, Graduate School Seoul National University, 2001.

Lewis, James Lee. "The Burmanization of the Karen People: A Study in Racial Adaptability." PhD dissertation, The University of Chicago, 1924.

Malseed, Kevin. "Networks of Noncompliance: Grassroots Resistance and Sovereignty in Militarized Burma." *The Journal of Peasant Studies* 36, no. 2 (2009): 365–391.

Marshall, Harry. *The Karen People of Burma: A Student in Anthropology and Ethnology.* Columbus: The University of Ohio, 1922.

Mason, Francis. *The Karen Apostle: Or, Memoir of Ko Thah-Byu, the First Karen Convert, with Notices Concerning His Nation.* Boston: Gould, Kendall, and Lincoln, 1843.

McBrien, J. Lynn. "Educational Needs and Barriers for Refugee Students in the United States: A Review of the Literature." *Review of Educational Research* 75, no. 3 (2005): 329–364.

McMahon, Alexander Ruxton. *The Karens of the Golden Chersonese.* London: Harrison, 1876.

Moonieinda, Ashin. *The Karen People: Culture, Faith and History.* Bendigo, Victoria: The Karen Buddhist Dhamma Dhutta Foundation, 2010.

Neiman, Amy, Eunice Soh, and Parisa Sutan. "Karen." *EthnoMed,* 1 July 2008. Retrieved 2 February 2011 from https://ethnomed.org/culture/karen/#:~:text=The%20Karen%2C%20pronounced%20Kah%2D%20Ren,known%20as%20Burma%20or%20Myanmar.

Nezer, Melanie. *Resettlement at Risk: Meeting Emerging Challenges to Refugee Resettlement in Local Communities.* New York: J.M. Kaplan Fund, 2013.

Oh, Su-Ann, and Marc Van Der Stouwe. "Education, Diversity, and Inclusion in Burmese Refugee Camps in Thailand." *Comparative Education Review* 52, no. 4 (2008): 589, 590–617.

Organista, Pamela Balls, Gerardo Marín, and Kevin M. Chun. *The Psychology of Ethnic Groups in the United States.* Los Angeles: Sage, 2010.

Ott, Eleanor. *Get Up and Go: Refugee Resettlement and Secondary Migration in the USA.* Geneva: UNHCR, 2011.

Petry, Jeffrey Louis. "The Sword of the Spirit: Christians, Karens, Colonialists, and the Creation of a Nation of Burma." PhD dissertation, Rice University, 1993.

Phan, Zoya. *Little Daughter: A Memoir of Survival in Burma and the West.* New York: Simon and Schuster, 2009.

Po, San. C. *Burma and the Karens.* London: Elliot Stock, 1928.

Poduthase, Henry. "Rigor in Qualitative Research: Promoting Quality in Social Science Research." *Research Journal of Recent Sciences,* no. 4 (2015): 25–28.

Rajah, Ananda. *Remaining Karen: A Study of Cultural Reproduction and the Maintenance of Identity.* Canberra: ANU Press, 2008.

Richardson, Laurel, and Elizabeth Adams St. Pierre. "Writing: A Method of Inquiry." In *The Sage Handbook of Qualitative Research,* edited by Norman K. Denzin and Yvonna S. Lincoln, 959–978. Thousand Oaks, CA: Sage Publications Ltd., 2005.

Rumbaut, Rubén G. "Ties that Bind: Immigration and Immigrant Families." *Immigration and the Family: Research and Policy on US immigrants* (1997): 3–46.

———. "Ages, Life Stages, and Generational Cohorts: Decomposing the Immigrant First and Second Generations in the United States." *International Migration Review* 3, no. 3 (2004): 1160–1205.

Rumbaut, Rubén G., and Kenji Ima. *The Adaptation of Southeast Asian Refugee Youth: A Comparative Study*. Washington, DC: US Department of Health and Human Services, Family Support Administration, Office of Refugee Resettlement, 1988.

Russell, Susan. "Between Hills and Plains: Power and Practice in Socio-Religious Dynamics among Karen." *Journal of the Royal Anthropological Institute* 12, no. 1 (2006): 242–244.

Smeaton, Donald. *The Loyal Karens of Burma*. London: K. Paul, Trench & Co., 1887.

Smith, Martin. *State of Strife: The Dynamics of Ethnic Conflict in Burma*. Washington, DC: Institute of Southeast Asian Studies, 2007.

———. *Burma: Insurgency and the Politics of Ethnicity* (2nd ed.). New York: St. Martin's Press, 2020.

———. *Fifty Years in the Karen Revolution in Burma: The Soldier and the Teacher*. Ithaca, NY: Cornell University Press, 2020.

South, Ashley. "Karen Nationalist Communities: The 'Problem' of Diversity." *Contemporary Southeast Asia: A Journal of International & Strategic Affairs*, no.1 (2007): 1–12.

———. *Burma's Longest War: Anatomy of the Karen Conflict*. Netherlands: Transnational Institute Burma Center Netherlands, 2011.

Stake, Robert E. *The Art of Case Study Research*. Thousand Oaks: Sage, 1995.

Thawnghmung, Ardeth Maung. *The Karen Revolution in Burma*. Singapore: ISEAS Publishing, 2008.

———. *The "Other" Karen in Myanmar: Ethnic Minorities and the Struggle without Arms*. New York: Lexington Books, 2012.

Tillmann-Healy, Lisa M. "Friendship as Method." *Qualitative Inquiry* 9, no. 5 (2003): 729–749.

"Travel Loan Services." *US Committee for Refugees and Immigrants*. Retrieved 4 June 2011 from https://uscripayments.org/#:~:text=When%20refugees%20are%20 admitted%20to,over%20a%20pre%2Ddetermined%20period.

Tun, Chit. "Myanmar Nationals Deported from US Arrive in Rangoon." *The Irrawaddy*, 27 August 2018. Retrieved 2 February 2021 from https://www.irrawaddy.com/news/burma/dozens-myanmar-nationals-deported-us-arrive-yangon.html.

"U.S. Refugee Admissions Program: Reception and Placement." *US Department of State*. Retrieved 20 May from https://2009-2017.state.gov/j/prm/ra/reception-placement/index.htm

Wilson, Jill H., and Audrey Singer. "Refugee Resettlement in Metropolitan America." Association of American Geographers, San Francisco, 21 April 2007. Retrieved 30 June 2022 from https://www.brookings.edu/wp-content/uploads/2016/06/20070421.pdf.

Worldwide Refugee Admissions Processing System (WRAPS), *Refugee Processing Center*, 2021. (No longer available online.)

Zan, Spencer. *Life's Journey in Faith: Burma, From Rags to Riches*. Bloomington, IN: Author House, 2008.

Zremski, Jeremy. "Laura Bush: A Hero to the Refugees from Burma." *The Buffalo News*. Retrieved 28 September 2011 from http://projects.buffalonews.com/long-reads/burma/laura-bush.html.

Index

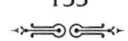